WITHDRAWN

DANIEL'S STORY

CAROL MATAS

SCHOLASTIC INC.
New York Toronto London Auckland Sydney
Mexico City New Delhi Hong Kong Buenos Aires

No part of this publication may be reproduced, stored in a retrieval system, or transmitted in any form or by any means, electronic, mechanical, photocopying, recording, or otherwise, without written permission of the publisher. For information regarding permission, write to Scholastic Inc., Attention: Permissions Department, 557 Broadway, New York, NY 10012.

ISBN-13: 978-0-590-46588-5
ISBN-10: 0-590-46588-0

Produced by Daniel Weiss Associates, Inc.
33 West 17th Street, New York, NY 10011

Copyright © 1993 by Carol Matas.
Cover art copyright © 1993 by Daniel Weiss Associates, Inc.
Cover painting by Paul Henry, based in part on a photograph by Mendel Grossman
All rights reserved. Published by Scholastic Inc. SCHOLASTIC and associated
logos are trademarks and/or registered trademarks of Scholastic Inc.

12 11 10 9 8 7 6 5   9 10 11 12/0

Printed in the U.S.A.   23

First Scholastic printing, April 1993

This book is dedicated to children everywhere in the hope that they will live in a world of peace and love, and to the memory of the children who found neither.

Contents

Acknowledgments

Heartfelt thanks to: Cassandre Aras, Donna Babcock, Rabbi Henry Balser, Amy Berkower, Per Brask, Rebecca Brask, Susan Kitzen, Nathan and Janeen Kobrinsky, Fran Lebowitz, Saari Matas, Sybil Milton, Susan W. Morgenstein, Morri Mostow, Perry Nodelman, Shirly Pinsky, Angela Reimer, Kate Waters, Dan Weiss, Alexandra Zapruder, and the United States Holocaust Memorial Museum.

EUROPE 1938–1939

● Important Cities

■ Concentration Camps 1933–1945

------- Daniel's Journey

PART ONE

PICTURES OF FRANKFURT

1

What has happened to me? I feel just like I did when I was around ten years old and I got hit by a soccer ball right between the eyes and I wandered around the field disoriented, not knowing who I was, where I was, where I should be going. I feel like that now—stunned and confused. Who am I? Where am I going?

This much I know. My name is Daniel. I am fourteen. And I am Jewish. I am on a train with my mother, father, sister, and what looks like over a thousand other Jews from Frankfurt. We do not have any idea where we are going, only that the Germans no longer want Jews in Germany. My country. Generations of our family have lived here going back a thousand years, but it looks as if we will be the last.

Father and Mother sit across from me and speak in low voices to each other. My sister, Erika, who at twelve is two years younger than I, sits beside me humming a tune to herself, no doubt composing a song for her violin. I bend over and pull my photo album out of my rucksack. I feel the need to look at my pictures, pictures of my life. Perhaps they can help me understand how I came to be on this train, who I am, and what has happened. I open the album to the first page.

The first picture in my album is that of me on my sixth birthday. Marked on the bottom is *March 30, 1933*. I am smiling at the camera, all pudgy cheeks and thick black wavy hair, my brand-new gleaming toy train on display in front of me.

Uncle Peter, my favorite uncle, would have taken this picture. He was the unofficial family photographer. The picture just beneath it is one he took later that day of our whole family. Everyone looks serious because they don't want to appear silly in the photograph. Still, I remember that day. The adults talking and laughing, the hustle and bustle as dinner was being prepared, the smell of freshly baked bread and roasting chicken, and, of course, the screaming and noise of all my cousins.

I look at each face in the photograph in turn. Uncle Peter isn't in the picture because he was taking it. He was married to Auntie Leah, my mother's older sister, a nurse. She always bossed us around and tried to organize our lives. Uncle Peter and Auntie Leah had four children under the age of five—Friedrich, a year younger than I, Mia, age four, Gertrude, age two, and Brigitte, age one. The children look so quiet and well behaved in the photo. But in reality they would run, scream, fight, and drive me crazy. I remember the first thing they went for when they got in the door that day was a magnificent castle I had made from my building set. I had labored over it for weeks, methodically snapping the pieces together until I thought it was perfect—it was demolished only seconds after their arrival. "Daniel," my mother *always* said to me just before they came over, "you are the oldest. You must hold your temper even if they do things you don't like." When I was five, I'd bopped Friedrich on the arm, hard, for breaking one of my toys. He'd cried. And ever since then all I'd heard was "You're the oldest." I looked at the shambles of my castle and felt like bopping them all. Strange, really, that they should be so wild, considering how strict Auntie Leah is. Perhaps she is better at controlling other people's children than her own.

Also in the picture is my mother's younger brother, David. He was an engineer and a bachelor, and we usually saw him at dinnertime, when he just happened to drop by to visit.

Standing beside my father are his three brothers: Leo, who came from Berlin with his family; Walter and Aaron, and their wives. Sitting on the floor are their children, three per family, most around my age or younger. I remember that as the photo was being taken Uncle Walter and Father were fighting, talking back and forth with clenched teeth so as not to ruin the picture.

"Palestine is the answer, Joseph," said Uncle Walter to my father. "We should all emigrate there."

"And do they need concert violinists in the Holy Land?" Father had replied. "No, Walter, they'll put you to work in the fields."

"Even a new country needs music," Walter retorted. "And the Jews need a country of their own."

"We have a country!" Father exclaimed. "Our

family has lived in Germany for over six hundred years. How long does it have to be before you call someplace home?"

"And my family," said Mother, and then the entire family joined in, *"has been here for almost one thousand years!"* Mother turned red. "Well, we have."

"We know!" Everyone laughed.

Auntie Leah spoke up. "It never hurts to be reminded."

Everyone laughed again. The picture had to be delayed while the adults put their serious faces back on.

Oma Rachel and Opa Samuel, my mother's parents, are in the picture too, as is Oma Miriam, my father's mother. Oma Miriam lived in an old-folks' home in Frankfurt, but was with us for my birthday. Opa Karl had died two years earlier. Right after the picture was finally taken, I remember Auntie Leah began to lecture me.

"Now, young man, I hope you'll work to deserve such a fine present. I understand your mother has just returned from *another* trip to see your teacher. It seems to me that she's called to your school at least once a week!" She looked at me sternly, and I was so mad I could have kicked her. She was always butting in! And it was so unfair! All I did in school was crack a few jokes and make some funny faces. My classmates thought I was funny and so did I. Why did my teacher, Mr. Schneider, have to be so sour? He always looked like he'd sucked on a lemon just before coming into the classroom.

"Leah, it's his birthday," Mother protested.

"I know, I know," Auntie Leah replied. "But you're too soft on him—he should realize how hard these meetings are on you."

"If Mr. Schneider wasn't so mean and stupid, I'd behave better!" I declared defiantly. Auntie Leah looked like she wanted to run over and cover her children's ears. They were all listening with great interest.

"You must show respect for your teachers, Daniel," she scolded.

"Why? They don't show respect for me," I shot back.

At that point Uncle Peter intervened.

"Who wants birthday candies?" he asked with a smile. I loved Uncle Peter.

"I wish *you* were my teacher, Uncle Peter," I said, giving him a kiss as he handed me a huge piece of chocolate toffee. "I'd never be bad in your class."

"No, Daniel, I'm sure you wouldn't. I agree with you, mutual respect is very important." Then he whispered in my ear, "But just to make things easier for your poor mother, maybe you could *pretend* a little respect."

I giggled and he gave me a wink. That made me feel so grown up that I decided to try it. Not that I could *always* control myself, but after that my mother visited Mr. Schneider every month or so instead of every week.

I stare at the next page and the next picture. Uncle Peter took this one two days after my birthday. It shows my father's hardware store. My father had a very successful business. People came to his store from all over, not so much for his merchandise, but for his advice. He knew how to fix anything and always took the time to show the people who came in what the best tools would be for a specific job. There was also a large section of household items like pots and pans and knives, and he would discuss the advantages of one over another with his customers as seriously as if they were deciding the fate of the world. That's why his customers would never consider shopping anywhere else—even if the price was a little cheaper. My mother worked in the back of the shop, doing all the accounting. I stare at the picture. Across the front window, written in large letters, is the word JEW.

I still remember when I first saw it. I was so confused. Jew. What was wrong with that? I went to a regular public school and most of my friends at school weren't Jewish, but that didn't matter. It was just a different religion. We lit candles on the Sabbath and went to synagogue—a reform synagogue where the service was mostly in German—and celebrated Jewish holidays. They celebrated Christian holidays. So what? But that day there wasn't only writing on the window. There was a storm trooper—Father said he was called a Brown Shirt because of the brown shirt of his uniform—and he was standing outside the door of the shop. With a gun! I had run there to help in the store, and then I didn't know what to do. I was scared.

I thought that maybe the storm trooper would shoot me if I got close. He looked so mean. And then Mrs. Werner came around the corner. She walked very slowly because she had to use a cane. She walked up to the man and said, "Excuse me, please."

The Brown Shirt looked at her and replied, "All Jewish shops are being boycotted. You can't go in there."

Mrs. Werner tapped his boot with her cane.

"Now you listen to me, young man. I walked a long way to get here. I'm ninety years old. Don't you tell me what I can and can't do!"

And the Brown Shirt stepped aside. I ran up to her and took her hand and we went in together.

"Daniel!" my father cried. "Mrs. Werner! You shouldn't have come. He might have hurt you!"

"Nonsense," she replied, and then went about her business. All she had needed was a light bulb!

I think back to that incident now and I wonder if the madness could have been stopped then. What if Father's regular customers had insisted, like Mrs. Werner, on being allowed in? Mrs. Werner wasn't Jewish and she didn't care that we were. But how many people had the courage to walk up to a young man holding a gun? What if he should shoot?

The next day the Brown Shirt was gone, and Uncle Peter came to the store to take the picture. As we stood in the street gazing at the shop, I asked him to explain what was happening.

"Have you heard of a man called Adolf Hitler?" Uncle Peter said.

"Of course!" I replied, insulted.

"Who is he?"

"He is chanskellur of Germany," I replied.

"Yes, Daniel, you mean chancellor, appointed by President Hindenburg. His party, the National Socialist party—they are called Nazis—has lots of seats in Parliament. Hitler has changed the constitution so that he now rules us. He can do anything he wants, Daniel, and the German people are happy to let him. They think he can solve all their problems of unemployment and that he can stop the fighting."

I nodded knowingly. I'd seen people fighting in the streets. "But why won't they let people shop in our store?" I asked.

"That's a good question, Daniel. Hitler wants

someone to blame all of Germany's troubles on, and he's decided it will be the Jews. And anyone else that isn't a 'pure' German of the 'Aryan' or 'master' race. I've heard they've opened up camps—they call them concentration camps—where they're putting all his enemies—communists, socialists, Gypsies, Jews, anyone who disagrees with him and anyone he doesn't like. And they are making sure everyone has heard of these camps—so people do not protest, for fear of getting arrested too."

"But," I said, "how can everyone love him so much if he's so mean?" I thought of the huge rallies Father had told me about, where tens of thousands cheered Hitler, and of the torchlight parades I'd seen many nights, in which his followers would march through town singing. I often felt like running out and joining the parades. They always looked so exciting.

"People think he will make Germany strong again—give it back its dignity. Come, let's go help your father wash that sign off."

The boycott of Jewish stores lasted only three days, and like any six-year-old, I quickly forgot all about it and went back to my happy life. My mother and father must have started to worry then, but they hid it well and I had other things to worry about—such as whether or not I would make the school soccer team and if I could convince Father to buy me the beautiful model car that was displayed in the shop window next to his.

2

I look at the picture on the next page—the last class photo taken just before I left public school. It is marked *Class of 1936/37.* What strikes me is all the faces *not* in the picture—my Jewish friends who had over the years either left voluntarily to go to Jewish schools or been forced to leave. I had wanted to stay at that school because my best friend, Hans, was there, and he wasn't Jewish. But slowly Hans began to find excuses for not coming over to my house, and he started to pick fights with me in the schoolyard. I always got in trouble for those fights, of course, because I was a Jew, a natural troublemaker, according to Mr. Schneider.

Just thinking about Mr. Schneider gets me mad all over again. One day, soon after my tenth birthday, he called me to the front of the class. He had a measuring tape, which he flung about in the air.

"Jews," he cried in his shrill voice, "are not our

11

equals. They never were. They bribed their way into positions of power. They tried to take over all our banks and financial institutions. They tried to take over our country. We must all thank God that He sent Adolf Hitler to us, for only he has had the courage to deal with this Jewish problem. Now the Jews are no longer citizens, they have no rights, and soon they will no longer pollute our schools."

I was torn between kicking him and throwing a desk at him, so for the moment I did nothing. He'd always been mean to me. Whenever I got an answer wrong, he'd say, "What can you expect from a Jew?" But he'd never gone on like this before.

"The authorities have instructed us to illustrate the inferiority of this race to you students in this way," Mr. Schneider continued. "True Aryans have specific head measurements." Before I knew it, he had the tape around my head. He quickly marked it and held it up triumphantly to the class. "You see! Inferior species. Head too small, no room for brains, a close relative to the vermin in our gutters."

That was it. I could take it no more.

"Good!" I exclaimed. "Because I'd hate to be like you!" And *then* I kicked him.

Everyone in the class gasped.

"Leave this room!" Mr. Schneider screamed, hitting me around the head and shoulders. "Go straight to the principal's office."

"I'll leave this room and I'll never come back," I screamed as I tried to duck the blows. I went straight to Father's store, and I pleaded with him to take me out of that school. The next day both Erika and I started in the Jewish school, about ten blocks from home.

This next picture shows me outside my new school, with Erika and Uncle Peter. Father took this picture. It is dated *April 1937*. It's amazing to look at it and to realize how little I understood then. I didn't care that I'd been virtually forced out of my own school. I was thrilled at the idea of never seeing Mr. Schneider again and delighted that Uncle Peter would be my new teacher.

Uncle Peter had been fired from his teaching job because he was Jewish—that's why he was now teaching at the Jewish school. Not only him; all the Jewish professors from the University had been fired—so we had very talented, knowledgeable teachers. It wasn't as much fun getting into trouble. The teachers looked at me with such disappointment when I did something stupid that I eventually stopped. And I started to enjoy myself. I discovered that with a good teacher, school could actually be interesting.

I look at this picture of the three of us smiling in front of the Jewish school and I realize that it was then that my life really began to change. I remember running home to tell Mother all about my first day at my new school.

Something in her face made me stop, as I chattered on about my new schoolmates, how good it was to have friends again, and what a good teacher Uncle Peter was.

"What's the matter?" I asked.

"What's the matter?" she replied, and suddenly her eyes blazed with fury. "I'll tell you what the matter is. Our family goes back a thousand years and yet you aren't German enough to go to public school. How dare they! That criminal Hitler isn't good enough to carry your books!"

I was so shocked, I didn't reply. Mother was always so calm, so quiet. She *never* got mad.

"Don't be mad, Mother," I said. "I *like* it there."

"I know you do, Daniel," she said, and I saw tears in her eyes, "but that's not the point." Then she sat down at the kitchen table and looked so sad I didn't know what to do. Slowly I backed away and went to my room. When I saw her at supper, she was back to her calm, quiet self and never mentioned it to me again.

Uncle David moved to the United States that summer. A few years earlier the Nuremberg laws had been passed, laws designed to "protect" German blood and honor. Jews were not allowed to marry Germans. Uncle David was engaged to a Christian woman, and they left Germany so they could marry. Those laws also took away citizenship from all Jews and their right to vote. Uncle David wanted us to join him in the United States, but my parents didn't want to leave Frankfurt. Still, lots of their friends were leaving. Every day Father announced a new name at the dinner table.

"You know the Cohens down the street? On their way to England. The Pearlmans, who have the clothing store near ours? Australia!"

Mother would shake her head. And then Father would say, "They'll be back."

Still, it felt to me like everything was changing too fast—and for the worse. It seemed there was a law for everything, most of them forbidding Jews to do the things I most enjoyed. We couldn't go to concerts or eat at restaurants or even swim in public pools. Big signs were posted at the pools saying "No Jews or Dogs Allowed." Still, I tried to convince myself that it wasn't that bad. My mother cooked better than any restaurant chef, and my friends and I played soccer after school. Very quickly the Jewish community banded together and organized its own Jewish cultural centers—Uncle Walter was fired from the Frankfurt Symphony, so he joined the Jewish Symphony. We even had our own community swimming pool. I made new friends and I joined a sports club sponsored by a Zionist organization. Zionists believed that Jews needed their own homeland, so along with martial arts and soccer, we also had lectures on how we would create the perfect Jewish state in Palestine. By the time I was eleven, I'd almost forgotten life had ever been different.

One night, though, I was reminded how different things really were. My friends Joshua and Mordechai and I were walking home from the Zionist sports club at around nine o'clock. We had been practicing martial arts all evening, but we weren't tired. A fresh layer of snow lay on the ground and we were feeling happy and full of energy. We threw snowballs and chased one another down the streets. We had paused at a street corner to say good-bye when four boys in Hitler Youth uniforms came up behind us. Perhaps they had followed us, I don't know. These were the "perfect Aryans," children training to be future leaders of Hitler's Germany—the Germany that had no place for Jews.

"Hey, Jew boy," one called, "didn't your mother ever teach you to wash?"

"Yours should wash your mouth out with soap!" I replied.

"Why, you . . . !" He turned red. Couldn't believe a Jew had actually answered him back. And then suddenly they were all over us. But even at their four to

our three they were no match for us. The blue-eyed
blond who'd taunted me was soon flat on his stomach,
his face in the snow.

"Give up?" I asked.

"No!" he screamed, struggling.

I sat on him hard and pushed his face farther into
the snow.

"Now?"

"Yes! Yes! Let me up!"

He scrambled up and raced off with the others.
The three of us laughed and joked about it, but as I lay
in bed that night, I knew that none of us had found it
fun—or funny. We were separate now from everyone
else in Frankfurt. Separate and somehow less important. Not as good as the "pure," "real" Germans. And
everywhere there were posters, exhibits, and articles
that described to the German people how terrible Jews
were. I *knew* I was no different from them, and yet
sometimes—I wondered.

In fact, I took Erika to see a newsreel about one of
those exhibits.

I look at the next picture. Little Erika standing with
her violin, staring seriously into the camera. Under it
is written *June 1938*. Erika was nine. A little mouse.
She had brown wavy hair and brown eyes and a little
nose that she would rub when she was worried. Uncle
Walter had begun teaching her violin when she was
only four years old because she'd begged and begged
him. From the moment she attended her first symphony to hear her Uncle Walter play, all she wanted to
do was learn the violin. She is so much like Mother—
quiet, calm—but she's also terribly shy. Everything
she feels she expresses in her music.

Shortly after this picture was taken, Erika and I

went to the movies. I wanted to go because I'd heard that before the feature they were showing a newsreel about a public exhibition called "The Eternal Jew," which was coming to Frankfurt. This exhibition was created for one purpose only—to convince German people of how disgusting Jews were. I just had to see it. I wanted to know what they were saying about us. I was looking after Erika, so I dragged her along. She was devastated by it. The newsreel described what was in the exhibit—a picture of Jews as slave drivers, thieves, and madmen, unlike the upstanding, honorable German people. I tried to laugh at it all, but inside I was terrified. Erika wept silently until I was so guilt stricken at having taken her that we got up and left. Auntie Leah waved to us from across the street.

"Daniel! Erika! I've been looking everywhere for you! Come on!"

Erika and I hurried over to her, relieved there was someone to take us home. I felt like everyone on that street knew we were Jewish, that they would gladly rip us to shreds or try to stamp on us as if we were bugs. Mother and Father were furious with me when they heard where I had taken Erika, and I was sent to my room for the rest of the day and evening.

That night I had a dream. In the dream Erika and I went to the movies and saw the horrible newsreel, just as we had that afternoon. When we came out, Auntie Leah called to us, her voice shrill, "Come on!"

Suddenly someone on the street yelled. "Hey, I know her. She lives near me. She's a Jew. Let's get her. Teach her a lesson." And then the people on the street moved as one as they went after her.

"Jew. Filthy vermin." They punched her and kicked her and then began ripping off her clothes.

"Run, Erika, run!" I screamed, and I pushed her away. Erika ran. I threw myself into the mob, screaming, "Leave her alone, leave her alone!" I punched and kicked, but they punched and kicked back. Finally Auntie Leah grabbed me, covered me up, threw her body over me, and went limp. Slowly the crowd lost its momentum and began to disperse.

Auntie Leah got up. Her clothes were in tatters. There was a terrible gash along her cheekbone, and two bottom teeth were gone.

"Daniel, are you all right?" she whispered. She was only worried about me. I started to cry. "I'm sorry," I said. "I'm sorry."

"It wasn't your fault," she said. Perhaps she thought I was apologizing for being in the wrong place at the wrong time. How could she know I was sorry that I'd never liked her and now this had happened to her and I still didn't know if I liked her, but I *knew*, I *knew* that no human being deserved to be treated that way—whether I liked her or not.

I kept repeating how sorry I was, and I took off my shirt and gave it to her. Father and Mother came with Erika, and then Mother started to cry. And I started to scream because I was scared, and how could this happen? Wasn't this Frankfurt? My home? And I screamed and screamed . . .

"Daniel, Daniel, wake up! You're having a nightmare!" My mother was holding me tight. "It's all right, sweetheart. You're safe. Nothing's going to hurt you. It's that movie," she scolded. "No wonder you're having nightmares."

The next day Father called a family conference to discuss what should be done about leaving or staying in Germany. Maybe he had started to realize that his children were going to grow up in fear. And he didn't want that for us.

Uncle Aaron announced he had applied for visas to England and that they would leave the moment the visas came through. He said we should all do the same.

"Now listen," Uncle Peter said, "for a thousand years Jews have survived pogroms, ghettos, and anti-Jewish laws, and we'll survive this. It's just more of the same. It'll pass."

"Maybe," Mother said slowly, "this is different."

"Ruth," Father said to my mother, "if it *is* different, we have to do something. It's time to think about going. David can sponsor us to go to the United States. Tomorrow you should go and fill out applications for our visas."

My mother nodded her head. And she did go the next day. But Uncle Peter was wrong that it would all just pass away. He was arrested a few days later for having pleaded guilty six years earlier to two parking violations. He was taken away to Dachau concentration camp.

Auntie Leah stared into nothingness as she told Mother what had happened. "He got those tickets when Brigitte was born. I was in labor and we couldn't find a parking place, so I screamed at him, 'Park illegally! We'll get a ticket, so what? Should I have the baby in the car, instead?' Oh God help us, what is happening?"

Oh God help us, what is happening?

3

I look up from my album to find my mother staring at me. It is warm in the train because it is so crowded, and Mother's face is flushed. Of course, it doesn't help that she is wearing two layers of clothes and her heaviest coat and her ski boots. Still, the flush on her cheeks just makes her look prettier. My friends were always telling me what a pretty mother I had, and all of Father's friends were taken with her the moment she walked into a room. She has dark wavy hair and large brown eyes; nothing unusual in that, it's just the way her face all comes together. She's not only beautiful, though, it's that her inner calm and sweetness shine through her eyes. I love to photograph her.

"What?" I say to her.

"It's your photo album," she replies. "When I was fourteen, Oma Rachel and Opa Samuel had pictures of all our special events—weddings, bar mitzvahs, anniversaries. . . . Look what your album has in it.

Nothing but horrible memories."

"They aren't all so bad, Mother," I say, trying to make her feel better. How can I tell her that I'm looking through them to try to make sense of this nightmare? I can't let her see how upset I am. It would only make her more miserable.

Her eyes well up with tears. She smiles in the hope that I won't notice. "Of course they aren't, Daniel."

She knows that I am trying to make her feel better, and that makes her feel worse.

"Why don't you close your eyes for a few minutes and rest?" my father suggests to her.

"Yes," she agrees. "I think I will."

She leans her head on Father's shoulder. Erika looks down at my album. She shakes her head when she sees the pictures I have it opened to, and goes back to composing quietly in her head.

I remember Auntie Leah giving me Uncle Peter's camera when she and her children moved in with us after they took Uncle Peter away. Friedrich settled into my room, and the first thing we did was turn one of the closets into a darkroom. Then I read every book I could on photography until I felt ready to begin taking pictures. Since Uncle Peter was my favorite uncle and Auntie Leah had given me his camera, I felt it was my duty to take over his responsibility as the family photographer. Friedrich and I made a pact that we would photograph everything we could as a record of our ill treatment by our fellow Germans.

I look at the photos of the identification cards we Jews had to carry. Our I.D. cards were stamped with a big *J* for Jew. If you didn't carry it at all times, you could be arrested, and yet if you did carry it you were marked as a Jew. The date on the photo reads *July 23, 1938.*

Erika suddenly interrupts my thoughts.

"Just after you took that, we had to change our names," she remarks, pointing at the I.D. card photos. The Germans, in their search for "racial purity," decreed all Jews had to add a Jewish name to their other one—Sara for a girl, Israel for a boy. If I signed anything, I had to sign it Daniel Israel. Father was Joseph Israel, mother was Ruth Sara, and Erika was now Erika Sara.

I remember Erika said at the time that Sara was a beautiful name and she was proud to add it to her own. Still, we should have seen then how much they really hated us, hated us so much that we couldn't even have German names. We had to be identified as Jews above all. But weren't we German, too? No more. This was another way to separate us from the "true" Germans.

The next photo is very underexposed. It shows Father's store, but this time the windows have been smashed, and it shows people leaving the store, arms filled with merchandise. These people were looting his store, carrying away whatever they could. They were Father's customers. People he trusted. It is the day after Kristallnacht, "the night of broken glass," called that because all night you could hear the sound of glass breaking, the glass of synagogues and Jewish stores and homes and prayer halls. Under the picture is the date *November 10, 1938.*

Father told me later that the events of that night had started in Paris, when a young Polish Jew had shot a German official. He did it to avenge his family, who had been expelled from Germany by the Nazis with thousands of others and sent without food, money, or any of their belongings to a city in Poland called Lodz. After the man he shot died, the SS, Hitler's elite bodyguards and powerful police force, ordered its troops into the streets of all German cities to take action against the Jews, to teach them a lesson. What a terrifying night it was.

We lived in a quiet residential area. We had both Jewish and non-Jewish neighbors. Our area was not deeply affected by the rioting, but Father had been working late and didn't return home that night. Fires blazed all over the city, glass broke, screams filled the air. My mother would let none of us leave the house. We turned off all the lights and pretended no one was home. We were in a panic, worried sick about Father. The next morning she allowed Friedrich and me to go search for him. We ran to the store. That's when I took this picture. But Father was nowhere to be seen. All that day we waited. Even Erika's violin was silent. Barely anyone spoke. Uncle Walter came over with Uncle Aaron. They sat with Mother. She cooked our meals and never broke down once.

Finally, at around nine P.M., the door opened—it was Father! Mother flew into his arms. I wanted to do the same, but suddenly I felt shy. He motioned Erika and me to come over, and gave us both a kiss. His brothers hugged him. Auntie Leah hugged him. He sank into a chair. Mother ran to get him a glass of water.

"I've been at the police station," he said softly. "I managed to bribe my way out. I don't want to talk about it." He turned to his brothers. "It's time to leave," he said. "Past the time."

"And what country will take us?" Walter said. "Remember that newspaper headline this summer after the conference at Evian in France? 'Jews For Sale. Who Wants Them? No One.'"

"Still," Father answered, "we must try."

Jews for sale. No one wanted us. The Germans
would have gladly let us go, but no country would
open their doors to us. They got together at a
conference and decided that they didn't want us any
more than Germany did. Yes, they took a few—just
not *too* many. Father tried hard to get us visas, but
many countries had decided that they would let in a
certain number of Jews each year, that many and no
more—they called it a quota. The United States had
a quota of people from Germany that was not filled,
yet they wouldn't let any more in either. Uncle
David, who was already in the United States, tried to
help us, but his letters became more and more dis-
couraged.

Most of the synagogues burned down during Kristallnacht. And many of the smaller prayer halls. After
that night, life became harder and harder. Father's
store was taken over by the Germans. They paid him
a few marks to make it all seem nice and legal, and a
man called Mr. Schnerr was given ownership of it.
Father was heartbroken. He'd worked all his life to
build up that business, and suddenly it was taken away
from him. Mr. Schnerr kept father on as a clerk—that
way the customers continued to come. Now we had
almost no money. Auntie Leah managed to get work
as a nurse at a Jewish hospital.

We were no longer even allowed to vacation in Germany—to go to the sea to swim or to the mountains to
ski. How I had loved skiing—the speed, the cold, the
daring. Mother had bought all of us brand-new ski
boots. They stood idle in the back hallway.

The next few pages of the album are a series of
photos I took on the streets of Frankfurt. To earn
money, I'd snap a picture and then ask the person if

he wanted to buy it. If he said yes, I'd take down his name and address and deliver the photo to him when it was ready. I was able to make a little money that way, and I also felt like I was recording these faces, and that behind each of these faces was a story, even if I didn't know it. Of course, the photos in my book are those that weren't bought. I look at a well-dressed gentleman, fear written all over his face. He was Jewish and he was terrified of me and my camera. Why had I taken his picture? Who was I working for? It shows how bad things were then—a twelve-year-old boy takes an adult's picture and the adult is terrified. Of course, children *were* dangerous—just down the street from us a Hitler Youth boy turned in his own parents to the authorities because his father was a socialist, a political enemy of Hitler's. They were sent to a concentration camp, and the boy was placed in a "good" home. I remember his parents well. They always had a smile for me and were quite friendly with Father and Mother.

Here is a picture of one of Mother's ration cards. After France and Great Britain declared war on Germany, in September 1939, we could buy food only with these cards. Our groceries became very limited. But Mother was a wonderful cook and a really talented baker—she could whip up anything with a bit of flour. I remember one day creeping into the kitchen, powdering my face with flour as she and Erika were working, and then shouting "Boo" at them. Mother knocked over the bowl she was so shocked, and Erika spilled the milk. They both scolded me terribly, but inside I enjoyed it. It felt good to be scolded about something ordinary like that—I think it made me feel that things *were* ordinary.

But nothing was ordinary or simple. When the war began, my friends and I were so confused. Some wanted Germany to win, others to lose, figuring that was the only way to get rid of Hitler. I was one of the ones who wanted us to lose, but that felt so wrong— everything was upside down.

I look at the next picture. It is one I took of Oma Miriam at the Jewish old-folks' home. She is staring seriously into the camera, her hair still black, only flecked with gray, her dark eyes boring into me. She wanted to move there after Opa Karl died. She didn't want to burden us, she said, by coming to live with us. She was funny and smart. I loved her. She did the strangest thing. When I think back on it now, it strikes me as so bizarre. But then, as a twelve-year-old boy, it seemed wild and wonderful. She made me a Hitler Youth uniform. I'll never forget the day she gave it to me. It looked almost exactly like the real thing. I gazed at her in disbelief.

"What is this?" I said.

"What does it look like?" she retorted.

"It looks like a Hitler Youth uniform," I replied.

I suppose I must have given her a rather odd look, because she smiled then and said, "No, Daniel, I'm not crazy. I know you. You're a free spirit. To tame you would kill you. I don't want that. You'll have to be strong, Daniel. And wild. And untamed." She paused. "Wear it. Go places you wouldn't be allowed to go. Have the freedom it gives you. And take that camera along. Record things. For history."

I was so astonished, I don't think I said anything. I just took it and left.

I hid the uniform in plain brown paper under my mattress so Mother wouldn't find it when she cleaned.

I would change into it on the days when the house was empty—Mother out trying to find food, everyone at school or work. I would double back from my way to school, go home, change, and then go out and enjoy Frankfurt.

I remember the first time I put it on and looked at myself in the mirror. My black hair tucked into the cap, with my blue eyes and fair skin I looked every inch the perfect Aryan. It gave me the strangest feeling. When I went out in the street, people often walked as far away from me as possible. I took my camera and took pictures of Jewish shops that had been taken over, of troops marching through the streets, even of exhibits of downed enemy war planes. I also took advantage of the freedom the uniform gave me to go to movies and museums, places I normally wouldn't be allowed to go into. My heart always pounded and I was sure I'd be discovered, but the uniform was a passport to freedom, just as Oma Miriam had promised.

One afternoon in early March I was walking across a small square near the center of town. I was in my uniform. Two SS Black Shirts were harassing and humiliating a group of Jewish men. Often the Nazis would go to Jewish homes and drag the men out or just find them on the street and pick on them.

A wooden platform had been erected in the square, and four men, all about Father's age, were sitting on stools. Around their necks were signs reading "Violated the Spirit of National Socialism" or "Insulted Our Way of Life." A crowd had gathered, and they taunted these men. Some threw rotten tomatoes. The men could not defend themselves, could not even wipe the rotten fruit from their faces.

Suddenly one of the Black Shirts noticed me. "Hey, you," he called. "Come here with that camera. Have a look at our show-and-tell."

I walked over, forcing myself not to tremble, not to look afraid.

"Take a picture of these idiots," he laughed.

"With pleasure," I agreed, my voice louder than normal so he couldn't tell how terrified I was.

"You take that picture to your youth group," the Black Shirt told me. "Your instructor will be very proud of you. Now that's *real* show-and-tell."

"Yes, I will, thank you," I said. I took another one just to make sure he thought I was enthusiastic enough, and then hurried away. Tears burned in my eyes. I knew one of the men. He was a distant cousin of mine. He hadn't even recognized me in my uniform. I don't have those pictures. I know I should have kept them for my records, but when I saw them after they'd been developed, I ripped them to shreds in a fury of disgust.

And then I put the uniform away. I realized that even though it gave me freedom, I had to be who I was—Daniel, a twelve- almost thirteen-year-old Jewish boy who carried an I.D. card stamped with a big red *J*. But now I understood what all those non-Jewish boys who wore the uniform felt. The uniform gave them power, respect, and freedom. It must have been terribly exciting. How easy for them to put on the uniform and with it all of Hitler's ideas, forgetting any moral standards they might have had. After all, the whole country loved (and feared) them. Surely there could be nothing wrong in that! And who told them anything different? Their teachers, their parents, those who should have told them right from wrong, told them wrong was right.

Not long after that, Mother discovered the uniform one day when she was making my bed. When I admitted what I'd been up to, she and Father were furious. Father dragged me to Oma Miriam's room at the home and confronted her.

"What could you have been thinking of?" he exploded. "He could've been killed."

"He wasn't, was he?" she replied calmly.

He was *so* angry. He glared at her. "No thanks to you," he said, and he stomped off. She gave me a wink as he dragged me behind him.

I pat her picture. She killed herself a month later, just after my thirteenth birthday. She saved up the sleeping pills they gave her each night. One evening, she took them all, went to sleep, and never woke up. But she made sure to come to my bar mitzvah first. It was held at a small prayer hall. Uncle David was gone, married now and living in the United States, and Uncle Aaron and his family had left for England. Uncle Leo couldn't come from Berlin because his family had no money for the trip. And, of course, I couldn't help but miss Uncle Peter. I'd always thought he'd be there at my bar mitzvah. A few of Father's friends came, and all my classmates. It wasn't the celebration I had once imagined, just a small, quiet marking of my entry into Jewish manhood and all its responsibilities.

Oma Miriam had left a note before she died. It said, "Please don't be angry. I've had a good life. I fear what is ahead. I don't want to suffer and I don't want to see you suffer. I go in peace."

I read those words over and over and over. I was angry. So angry. I wouldn't talk to anyone for a

week. Not even Erika, who tried to console me. But
I'm not angry anymore. Thank God she didn't live to
see us thrown out of our homes and out of our
country. And right now that's all I can thank God for.
Not much, is it?

4

I close my photo album. I don't have pictures of the most important things that happened over the next year—how can you take pictures of such terrible things? But I can see them in my head like photos, the expressions on people's faces, the backgrounds, everything.

One day a few months after Oma Miriam died, I answered the door and a postman asked me to sign for the parcel he was delivering. I signed and took it into the house with much curiosity. Mother and Auntie Leah ran over, excited. All the children gathered around. A parcel. Perhaps a friend was sending us food, special treats, or clothes for the children. Or maybe it was from Uncle David or Uncle Aaron. But no, the postage was German. In fact, as I looked closer, I realized it was from Dachau.

"It's from Uncle Peter!" I exclaimed.

I ripped it open. Auntie Leah's face was full of

expectation. We had not received a letter from him for one full year. He'd been arrested two years ago, and at first he'd written all the time. Then he'd had a friend from the camp write to tell us that he'd gotten into some kind of trouble, and instead of letting him out, as they did with most of the people who were there for petty offenses, he was being held. And that was the last thing we'd heard. Auntie Leah was afraid he'd tried to organize the prisoners against their jailers or had become a spokesman for them.

A small box tied with string was inside the wrapping. And a note. Auntie Leah grabbed the note; I tore open the box. But what was this? Was it a strange joke of Uncle Peter's? Sending us a box full of ashes?

Auntie Leah started to scream. Mother took the note from her and read it. She looked at the children, who were starting to cry because their mother was so upset.

"Daniel, take the children to their room. I'll be there in a minute." Auntie Leah was screaming and crying. I still couldn't understand what was happening. And then finally it dawned on me. I hustled the children into their room. They were all crying, even Friedrich. I sat them all down on the bed. "It's Father. He's dead, isn't he?" Friedrich sobbed.

I nodded. He was dead, and the Nazis had sent us his ashes.

I stopped taking pictures after Uncle Peter's death. I just didn't have the heart for anything after that. I dragged myself to school, but my marks dropped because I couldn't concentrate. I didn't want to study—what was the point? So I could grow up to be a teacher, an engineer, a lawyer? All those professions were banned to Jews. I couldn't see my future anymore. So many of my school friends were gone now—the lucky ones having left for other countries while they were still allowed to do so. Erika was no companion really. She became even more quiet and withdrawn, practicing her violin constantly. Friedrich was now my closest friend. I started to read a lot and would spend hours in my room with my books. My favorite one was *The Count of Monte Cristo*, which I read at least five times. I suppose in better times Mother and Father could have helped me more, but they were so upset themselves, they didn't see how unhappy I'd become. Mother spent all her time going from consulate to consulate, desperately trying to get us papers so we could leave the country. She must have tried the black market, too, because her mink coat suddenly was gone one day, along with some of her best jewelry. But nothing worked. We were stuck.

I almost failed school that year, and summer holidays came as a great relief. Slowly I started to feel better. I swam at the Jewish community swimming pool, played soccer, and sunbathed in our yard. Erika also perked up. She often brought girlfriends over, and they giggled and made eyes at Friedrich and me. We were both interested in a couple of fifteen-year-old girls at the sports club, but they thought we were too young. Still, the sun and the heat and the lazy days all made me feel better—and I guess the passing of time helped too. It still hurt when I thought about Oma Miriam and Uncle Peter—but not as much. Although I never stopped missing them.

When summer was over, I felt ready to get back to school, and I buckled down to my studies. But that September another law was passed. I can see them, just like in a photo, the yellow stars with the word *Jew* printed on them that we were all forced to wear on our clothes.

And then we got the news in October that we were to be deported. That meant we were to be forced out of our homes. All our property and our clothes were to be itemized and signed over to the authorities. We were told what we could and could not pack. Naturally they wanted anything of value, such as furs, good boots, or warm clothes. But Mother made sure we packed our warm things and took along lots of food. Father took money along in case he needed to bribe anyone. They marched us through the streets of Frankfurt toward the market hall. I felt so helpless—I couldn't do anything to stop any of it.

They crowded thousands of us into the cellars of the market hall to spend the night until the trains departed. And what happened there—I don't want to think about that. Will remembering this help me to understand? How can one understand this? They were so afraid that we might leave with something of value, they hated us and despised us so much, that they body-searched us all. Mother and Auntie Leah and Erika were searched. They couldn't cry out for help, couldn't complain, because then they'd be beaten as well. After that, Erika couldn't stop crying. She cried all night. And so did I. Because I couldn't do anything to stop them from hurting my mother and sister and aunt.

Now I look out the train window as we move farther and farther away from Frankfurt. My album is back in my rucksack, and we are traveling away from Frankfurt. Yes, I can see from going through these pictures how it all started slowly and then got worse and worse and how the German people didn't try to stop it and how slowly all our rights were taken away until we were nothing but bodies being shipped out. I am scared. Still, I've defied them by taking pictures and not listening to their rules, and I'll keep doing that. I will.

I close my eyes and try to rest. At least our family is together. Auntie Leah and her children are also on this train, and so is Uncle Walter's family.

We travel all day, and finally the train stops for good and we are roughly ordered off. I step out, carrying my rucksack and my suitcase, and I can't believe what I see. It is cold and raining and before us is a wasteland of mud. Old buildings and slums loom in the distance.

"Where are we?" I ask.

"Just a minute," Father says, "let me find out." He comes back soon. "We are in Lodz, Poland. They've moved all the Jews into a ghetto here. That is where we are going."

German guards push us over to wagons, where we are told to deposit our belongings.

"Keep everything you can carry with you," Father orders. "Who knows if we'll ever see any of it again, otherwise."

So we trudge with the others from the train toward our new home in the ghetto of Lodz, Poland.

DENMARK SWEDEN Baltic Sea LATVIA

North
Sea

LITHUANIA

EAST
PRUSSIA

THE NETHERLANDS

■ Chelmno

Berlin ●

GERMANY

●Warsaw

U.S.S.R.

BELGIUM

● Lodz

Buchenwald ■

POLAND

● Weimar

Frankfurt ●

Nuremburg ●

■ Auschwitz

FRANCE

● Prague

CZECHOSLOVAKIA

Dachau ■

Munich ●

Vienna ●

AUSTRIA

● Budapest

SWITZERLAND

HUNGARY

ROMANIA

ITALY

YUGOSLAVIA

Belgrade
●

Adriatic
Sea

Mediterranean Sea

EUROPE 1938–1939

● Important Cities

■ Concentration Camps 1933–1945

-------- Daniel's Journey

BULGARIA

ALBANIA

PART TWO

PICTURES OF LODZ

5

How long has it been since that last train ride? Almost three years. We left Frankfurt in October 1941, when I was fourteen, and now it's August 1944, and I'm seventeen. I suppose I'm lucky to have lived this long.

Again I am on a train. Again I don't know where I'm going, only where I'm coming from. We left Lodz at around four o'clock this afternoon.

The Nazis told us we were going to a work camp, but I know that, for the Nazis, lying is as natural as murder. People moan, children cry for water; there is only an open bucket for a toilet, and the stench is unbearable. Unbearable. What a word. Is there nothing we haven't learned to bear? A hundred people are packed into this closed freight car, and I know that many won't survive if this trip is a long one.

I think back to that first train trip, the one from Frankfurt to Lodz, and how terrible I thought it was.

But now, stuck in this freight car, I know what true terror and misery are. I didn't bring my album. But I brought some of my pictures. The rest I hid.

Memories. Pictures. That's all I have left. How will they murder me? A shot in the head? Buried alive in a pit? Some other way I cannot even imagine?

No. I will not spend my last hours dwelling on that. The train rocks and sways. I lean against the filthy wall and jealously guard my spot. A small crack in the wood allows a faint beam of light to sift across my hands. I look at the pictures I have just removed from my boot. They are so worn and I have looked at them so often, I can tell them apart almost by their feel—this one of Erika and me has a small piece torn off the corner, this one of Rosa is frayed at the bottom, and on and on. But I don't want just to feel them, remember them; I want one last look, one last good look. I will go over them one by one, and I will remember.

I look at the first picture, the ray of light slanting across it. I know this one so well. Mother and Father and Erika have looked at it so often that it is practically wrinkled.

I call it the Family Reunion. We are all there—except Uncle Aaron and his family and Uncle David and Aunt Lotte. Uncle Leo and Auntie Anna, and their children Nathan, Jakob, and Georg, arrived in Lodz from Berlin just after we arrived. Auntie Leah is there with her four children; Uncle Walter and Auntie Hannele and their three children; Oma Rachel and Opa Samuel. No one is smiling. Erika is twelve in this picture and very pretty.

The Jewish authorities, who were forced by the Nazis to organize the ghetto, put us in an old school. There were about sixty people per room. We slept on wooden planks and were given soup from a soup kitchen that was set up. We still had food with us— Mother had insisted on bringing all the food we could carry. She'd also insisted that we pack our warmest clothes, and our best winter coats, and wear our ski boots! I had laughed. "Ski boots, Mother?" I'd teased. "I don't think they're sending us on holiday."

"What are the warmest boots you own?" she'd asked.

"The ski boots," I'd admitted. They were also practically brand-new, as we'd never had the chance to wear them—I'd grown into Father's and Erika had grown into mine by the time we left. Mother and Father took their old ones. I'm wearing Father's now. They still have no holes in them. They may have saved my life. While others tried to struggle through the winters in shoes, we had warm boots.

Sometimes when it was winter in Frankfurt I'd run out to do something with my friends, leaving my winter coat behind on purpose. It was the fashionable thing to do in our age group—coats were considered strictly for adults. Mother used to scold me and swear I'd catch pneumonia. I never did. I enjoyed the cold, boasted to my friends how red my feet were, how little I needed to wear when I was outside. But how different to be running from one warm house to another than to be trapped day and night in an unheated school when the temperature is twenty-five degrees and people are suffering from frostbite and malnutrition. We'd been there only a week when our own food supply ran out. Many people in the school started selling their clothes for food. Uncle Leo did that, thinking that at any minute these conditions would improve. Father forbade any of us to sell anything.

"We don't know how long we will be here," he said one night at a meeting of the entire family in a corner of one of the large, cold rooms. "We must behave prudently at all times. Never lose our heads. Keep all your warm clothes. Ration your food carefully. We are given one loaf of bread each, which must last us six days. No one is allowed to finish that loaf on the first or even the second day. It *must* last or by the end of the week we could easily starve."

Starve. Everyone shifted uncomfortably. And yet we knew it was true.

The shock of what we saw when we first entered the ghetto will never leave me. People were actually starving to death. Lodz was a city that had hundreds of thousands of Jews in it before the war. Many fled east when the war began; the rest had been pushed into the poorest, dirtiest area in the city. They had tried to clean it up to make it habitable, but it would never be anything but a slum full of old apartment buildings and small wooden houses, only a few with running water, heat, or plumbing. Many streets were made of mud, and you sank into it when you walked. The smell of all those people crammed together in a such a small area with no sanitation was terrible. Over that winter, people died in the streets and lay unburied for days.

And Uncle Leo, who had stubbornly refused to listen to Father, sure that things would improve, learned that Father had been right when his youngest son, Georg, developed frostbite in his hands and feet because Leo had sold some of their warm clothes. The frostbite got infected. Georg got thinner and thinner. We all did, of course. When all you have to eat is a few ounces of bread a day and a bowl of soup, what can you expect? One cold February night Georg went to sleep and never woke up. We had to wait three days for them to come and bury him because the waiting list was so long. Three days. Auntie Anna didn't cry. She just sat with him day and night until they took him away. After that she seemed to lose the will to live. She got thinner and thinner and one morning she too didn't wake up. We were surrounded by death. I remembered when one death would be such a tragedy the whole community would mourn. Life was normal, death for a young child or an adult in middle age was not. But suddenly everything was wrong, upside down. It seemed more normal to die than to live.

I look at the picture again. So few of us are left. In the spring the Germans decided to ship out most of those newly arrived from Germany once again. Transports from Lodz had been leaving all winter. They were dreaded because people didn't know where they were going, but they feared the worst.

And then the notices came for Uncle Leo and his two sons and Uncle Walter and his whole family and Auntie Leah and her children, but not for us. Because Father was a World War I hero, he was exempt. The Jewish authorities in charge of housing found us an apartment, and we were finally able to move out of the school. Father begged them to let Oma Rachel and Opa Samuel stay with us. And he begged for the rest of the family too. In the end they let Oma Rachel and Opa Samuel stay. And Auntie Leah was able to convince them she could be of use to them as a nurse, so they let her and her children stay. The others were shipped off. I remember the hugs and kisses, the tears. We never heard from any of them again. Are they all dead? Or have they somehow survived until now, like us? I don't think the Nazis will let any of us survive. If they can manage to finish the job, they will.

I can see the next picture, just faintly in the light. It is a picture of a radio. To me this picture is not just of a radio but a symbol of defiance. Resistance. All radios had been banned to Jews in Frankfurt years earlier, but Father refused to hand ours in. He kept it hidden in the basement and we would listen for news of the war secretly, in the cellar. He couldn't take it with us when we left—he knew we'd be searched. But when we arrived in Lodz, one of the first things he did was trade a box of noodles for a radio from a local resident. Of course, this radio too was illegal, but when we moved into our apartment we found it had a small cupboard built into the wall. We put a bed in front of the cupboard, and the radio inside it. As the war dragged on, we listened to broadcasts in German from the BBC. Father knew that we could all be deported or shot if they discovered the radio. But he also knew that hope was as important as bread—perhaps more important. It gave us some dignity knowing that in this small way we were breaking the rules and defying them. Father also had a small diary thrown in as part of the deal for the noodles. He gave it to me. I wrote in it when I could, as a supplement to my pictures, as a further record I hoped would survive the war.

We counted ourselves fortunate. We had our own apartment—only one room—which we shared with Opa Samuel and Oma Rachel. Mother had managed to get a job at a bakery and was able to bring home a loaf of bread every few days. A loaf had to last each person seven days by then, and this extra bread gave us enough energy to carry on. Also, since we were all working, we managed to get enough ghetto money to buy vegetables and canned meat when they were available. Our rations were a vast improvement over those we were given while we were stuck in the school. We made sure that Auntie Leah and my cousins always had some to share as well. They also had a room in our apartment block. We were on the second floor; they were on the first. Because Mother was so frugal and clever at stretching our rations, none of us were yet suffering from the effects of starvation. Not that we weren't always hungry and often weak. We were. Father worked in a carpentry workshop, I worked at a metalworks factory in an apprenticeship program, and Erika worked at a sewing factory. Everyone worked. That's what the ghetto was for. Slave labor. Those who didn't work were deported out. Oma Rachel worked sorting feathers and Opa Samuel, who had been a dentist before he retired (he was already seventy-five), worked at the hospital.

And then Oma Rachel got sick. Auntie Leah was sure it was a form of starvation—Oma's legs swelled up and she couldn't walk. She had terrible rashes on her skin that quickly got infected. She developed a fever. Opa Samuel realized that she'd been secretly giving away her food—to us. She'd add a slice of bread to the family stock, or her ration of vegetables would find its way into someone's soup bowl. That was Oma Rachel. Everyone came before her. She had always fussed over us all and spoiled us. I remember the huge glass bowl of candy she'd kept in her house, and whenever we went to visit, we always were urged to eat as much as we could. And her husband a dentist! He used to scold her about it, but she never listened. How my mouth waters thinking of those soft toffees and those tart hard lemon rocks.

Auntie Leah and Opa Samuel used all the pull they had in the hospital and managed to get Oma a bed. This was a great triumph. It was almost impossible to get a bed in the hospital. She was given some vitamin injections and everyone hoped she would be all right.

And then one morning, as I was working in the shop, terrible news spread from one person to the next. There were gasps and cries and people left their work and ran. I remember that, even though it was September, it was terribly hot. We'd been in the ghetto almost a year by then, and I'd seen terrible things— but I was unprepared for what happened next.

"What is it?" I asked a small group that had gathered by the door.

"They're evacuating the hospital."

Oma. Oh no. All I could think of was to run, to get there, to try to save her. It didn't take a genius to realize that they weren't evacuating the hospital to take all these sick people to a work camp. There could be only one reason—they were too sick to work and therefore they must die. I ran along the narrow crooked streets with throngs of others. And when I neared the hospital, I saw that I was cut off. Hundreds of policemen and guards kept people well back from the hospital.

It was a pitiful sight. Those who could walk were pushed out into the waiting trucks; others were carried out in stretchers. I could see people trying to escape, some running, some jumping from the windows. Everywhere around me people screamed, called out to relatives hoping at least to say good-bye, see them one last time, but we couldn't, we were too far away. And then, the worst . . . German soldiers threw babies, newborns, little children, out of the windows and into the trucks below. I could stand no more. I turned, weeping, and stumbled back to our apartment. And who was there? Oma Rachel! Wearing a white gown and holding a surgical mask in her hand.

She grinned at me. "I had to think fast, Daniel. But I kept my head. I grabbed this and walked out as if I were a doctor." Soon the whole family was there, and despair turned to joy on each face as they walked in and saw Oma Rachel.

But the next morning, before we had even gotten up, there was a terrible banging on the door. And when we opened it, a policeman stood there and demanded that Rachel Aronsohn go with him to the transport.

"No!" Father objected. "She is all better. It's true she was at the hospital, but she's fine now."

"That may be," the policeman answered, "but it's no concern of mine. We have strict orders to take her. We are taking everyone who was listed at the hospital yesterday."

Father begged and pleaded, but it did no good. And then Opa Samuel got his things together and hers and announced that they would go together.

"No!" Father cried.

Opa Samuel gave Father a big hug and kiss. "We've been together all our lives. Should I let her go off alone now?"

So Father had to let them go. I felt so sad, I thought my heart would break. Of course, I'd felt terrible when little Georg died and Auntie Anna. But I hadn't known them well, hadn't grown up with them. Hadn't loved them the way I loved Opa Samuel and Oma Rachel. I only hoped that Oma and Opa wouldn't be made to suffer too much. But if they were sent on a trip like the one I am on now, that hope was in vain.

Still, the worst was not over yet. Oh no! Two days later the chairman of the ghetto made a terrible announcement. All children under ten and all old people were to be sent away. Again it was obvious that only those who could work for the Germans would be saved. But these deportations would also take people who were working but who looked weak or frail—those who obviously soon wouldn't be able to work. There were rumors that those who were deported were taken to a place call Chelmno, where they were killed.

We had a family meeting in our apartment. Mother, Father, Auntie Leah, and myself. Erika looked after the children downstairs.

"They may well take Erika," Mother said. "She's thin and pale and small for her age."

Erika was actually very strong, but she didn't look it.

"Friedrich, too," Auntie Leah said. "He's just like Erika. Small and skinny, and with that rash on his face. . . . And what about Gertrude? She's only ten. And Brigitte. She's nine. They'll certainly take them. Only Mia is tall and healthy looking." Tears came to Auntie Leah's eyes. She fought them back. "I won't let them take my children," she said quietly.

"We can hide two in the cupboard," Father suggested. "It'll be dangerous. Almost no air. If they're in there too long . . ."

Mother nodded. "Dangerous. But maybe their only chance. The police will search the apartment. They'll have to be quiet. Not a word."

"So, Gertrude and Brigitte?" Father said.

"No," Auntie Leah replied, much to my surprise.

"They're too young. They'll get scared. They'll cry out. And then they'll be caught, and so will Erika and Friedrich. It must be the older children. Only they have a chance."

Father sighed. Were they choosing who would live, who would die? How do you make those choices about your own children? What if Erika and Friedrich suffocated in the cupboard?

"Gertrude and Brigitte are big for their ages," Auntie Leah said. "Perhaps that will be enough." And quickly she got up and left.

All ghetto residents were ordered to stay indoors after five P.M. For days we were forced to stay home. The hunger was terrible, because we were deprived of our work rations and we were afraid even to go to the ration center for food, as people were being plucked off the streets and sent away. It was hot, too. Terribly hot.

News of the raids, when they began, spread like wildfire. We waited for them to get to us. I tried to read, but I couldn't concentrate. We tried to talk, but conversation died quickly. And then, one afternoon, Friedrich ran into our apartment. "They're coming!"

Swiftly we helped him and Erika into the little cupboard. We took off the door handle and covered it with tape Father had taken from the workshop. Then we placed the bed in front of it and covered the bed with a huge comforter. Trembling, we went downstairs, all of us rubbing our cheeks so they would have some color and we would look healthy. They ordered everyone into the courtyard, and the Gestapo—the Nazi secret police—barked orders at us to line up. There was no medical inspection, as I had heard there had been in other streets. Just the whim of the Gestapo officer. He was a tall fellow, almost elegant. To him we were no more than insects. He sent people either to the right, away from the trucks, or to the left. Little children were ripped away from their parents, people wept and pleaded. The children cried, terrified. Our turn came. I stood up very straight and tall. I was sent to the right. So was Mother. So was Father. All the time I was listening for sounds from the apartments, because other police were searching them for hidden children. And then it was Auntie Leah's turn. She too was spared. As was Mia. But Gertrude and Brigitte were sent to the trucks. Auntie Leah ran after them and grabbed their hands.

"You may not go with them," the Gestapo officer said.

"I will not leave them," Auntie Leah replied.

"You must."

"I will not." She held on to their hands. Casually the officer raised his pistol and shot. First the two girls, then Auntie Leah. In the head. Mia screamed and ran toward them. Mother ran for Mia, but Father pulled her back because Mia was already too far away. The Gestapo officer gestured with his thumb at Mia and the police threw her into the truck. She was crying, "Mama, Mama," and then the truck drove away and the Gestapo officer left, and we were alone in the square with the other survivors.

Mother ran to Auntie Leah and the girls. She sank to her knees. She didn't cry. She just stared at them. Father went after her. And I thought of Erika and Friedrich. I turned and ran back to the apartment. I took the steps two at a time, barreled through the door, pulled back the bed, scraped the tape away, and reattached the door handle, my hands trembling. I opened the door and the two children tumbled out. They were weak and woozy, but alive. Mother ran in then and fell on them both, crying out, kissing them. Then Father came in. We sat and stared, and no one knew how to tell Friedrich he was an orphan. And that his two baby sisters were dead, the other deported from the ghetto. Finally Father said, "Friedrich, I want you always to remember that your mother was a true hero. She was brave and had the spirit of a lion." And then he told Friedrich what had happened.

A couple of days later the curfew was lifted. Twenty thousand people had been transported out of the ghetto. It was Rosh Hashanah, the Jewish New Year. Services sprang up everywhere, in little houses, in old sheds converted to prayer halls. And for ten days people prayed to God. As for me, I had always believed in God, but at that point I didn't know what to believe. What kind of God could allow such things to happen? I was angry. Angry at the world. I thought perhaps it was time for another flood—perhaps this was a species that didn't deserve to exist. And then I met Rosa.

6

The light slants across Rosa's picture. She has that funny little smile on her face, a smile that somehow conveyed "perhaps I shouldn't smile, perhaps you think it's inappropriate to smile, but I'll smile anyway." Her smile was an act of defiance all her own.

The picture is marked *December 1942.* I was fifteen then. It was taken a few weeks after I met Rosa—it took me that long to work up the courage to ask her permission to take her picture. I remember our first meeting so well—and find myself smiling even in this squalor, surrounded by death. All I knew by November of that year was work; work and somehow getting enough food to stay alive. The earlier years in Frankfurt, which we'd thought so awful then, seemed like a glorious dream. Mother and Father tried everything to balance our diet so we wouldn't get scurvy or beriberi or any other disease brought on by lack of vitamins. We also had to worry about tuberculosis, typhoid, typhus, and spotted fever. Typhus was spread by lice, and lice were everywhere in the ghetto. It was impossible *not* to have lice. The question was how many. Keeping clean was just as important in avoiding disease as eating. Every night before going to bed, Mother would insist that we each go through our clothes and clean the lice from them. They congregated in the seams. We would crush the lice and then make sure that we killed the eggs, too. There was no water for baths, so we could wash only in the sink. Also, we either had very little soap, which we used for dishes, or no soap at all. If we didn't kill the lice every night, they would multiply horribly.

One evening, as Father and Mother and I were delousing our clothes, and I was sitting in only my underwear, Erika burst into the room with a friend. She was so excited about introducing her new friend that at first she didn't notice what we were doing. Fortunately, Father still had his pants on, Mother her slip. I (who am naturally very white skinned) was beet red in about two seconds flat.

"Mama, Papa, Daniel, I have a friend you just have to meet!" Erika babbled. "We work together at the factory and she has started a youth group and she says I can attend even though I'm younger than everyone else!"

Well, I don't think I'd ever heard Erika say so much all at once in her entire life. Still, that wasn't my main concern at that moment. Two emotions were vying for dominance—shame and love. The shame was natural—not many fifteen-year-olds like to be caught in their underwear picking lice out of their clothes. Love. Well, that I can't explain. She was actually a little funny looking. She had bright red hair and pale skin with freckles and bright blue eyes and rather thin lips. But she was smiling. She was beaming. She was delighted to meet us. She shook all our hands, including mine, as if what she was witnessing were the most natural thing in the world.

And then, speaking in German, she said to me, "I used to watch monkeys at the zoo do this and think it was funny. Maybe God is watching us and thinks this is funny too."

She was still smiling, and yet I couldn't tell whether she was joking or not.

"I'm sorry," she said. "I've come at a bad time. But it was so nice to meet you all. Erika, please do bring your brother to the meeting."

And she was gone. I sat there staring after her for so long that I came out of my trance only when it registered that everyone was laughing at me. It was the first time I had seen Mother or Father or Erika laugh since that terrible September a few months earlier. Just for that I will be grateful to Rosa forever. In fact, they couldn't stop laughing. Mother was crying, she laughed so hard.

"I don't see what is so funny!" I objected. "Erika brings home a friend and humiliates us and all you can do is laugh!"

That set them off again. The more indignant I became, the harder they laughed. I didn't join in. I pretended to concentrate on the lice. But all I could think of was Rosa.

Very casually, after they had *finally* calmed down, I said to Erika, "When is this meeting Rosa mentioned? I *might* want to go."

And that started them all up again. Honestly! I

smile a little now, thinking of it. I certainly was love-struck. One look and I became moon-eyed.

I wanted to find out everything about her, but I knew if I asked anything more my family would only tease me, so I waited. She was probably from Poland, because she spoke to us in German, with lots of Yiddish words and phrases thrown in. Most Polish people, of course, spoke Polish to each other. Still, many of the Polish Jews also spoke both Yiddish and German. I had never learned Yiddish, but it was close enough to German that I picked it up quickly and used it at work. Father was the least proficient, but we all managed to get by. But that's all I knew about her. And that for some reason she could still smile. Maybe she was crazy. That was a possibility, of course. I wanted to find out.

The first meeting I went to was two evenings later. It was in a small, one-room house about four blocks over from our apartment house. Friedrich also came along. He was still living in the apartment where he had lived with his mother, along with a rabbi from Lodz who needed a place to stay. He could've moved in with us and he came up to see us every night, but he didn't want to leave his apartment. Perhaps he felt that to leave was to somehow desert his family; to leave was to finally admit they were all dead. We hoped that after a time he would begin to accept what had happened and come to live with us.

The first thing I noticed when I walked into the room was, of course, Rosa. The second was shelves full of books. The ghetto had a lending library that I went to often, as I loved to read, but this was different. I looked at the titles. They had novels by Thomas Mann and plays by Bertolt Brecht, both banned

authors and almost impossible to get hold of. I felt
like I had entered a fantasyland.

Rosa came up behind me.

"They're real, all right. Go on. Take one. You can
borrow it, bring it back next time, then borrow another." I took *The Magic Mountain* off the shelf.

Rosa grinned.

"I think you'll like it. Although any mention of food
is a painful reminder. It's hard to imagine, isn't it,"
she continued, "that somewhere in the world people
are going about their lives, eating, sleeping, laughing,
crying . . . ." She paused and looked right into my
eyes. "Falling in love."

I gazed back at her. Had I heard her correctly? Did
she mean anything by it? Then she flashed me a grin,
which she followed with a wink! I was so confused
that I didn't know what to say or how to respond. Was
she being romantic, was she teasing, was it both? I
think my face was bright red again. She was probably
expecting some witty reply from me.

"Daniel?"

When I spoke, my voice cracked.

"Hard to imagine," I replied like a dummy.

"Come and sit down," she said, and under her
breath she muttered, "before you fall down."

Quickly she introduced Erika, Friedrich, and me to
the rest of the group. There were seven others there,
four girls, three boys. They were in the midst of an
intense discussion about the different jobs the Jews
had to do to keep the ghetto from falling into chaos—
administering the food, health care, housing, and, of
course, police work.

"If the Jews refused to do these jobs," a young girl
said, "I wonder what would happen."

"I often wonder too," Rosa said. "Just imagine if we all got together and turned against the Nazis. Why can't people realize that this system only prolongs our suffering? We are a forced-labor camp. But in the end we will all still die—and in the meantime we will have helped the Germans. Look at all the uniforms and equipment we are making for the German war machine."

And then I heard Erika's voice. I couldn't believe that she would speak up in this group of strangers.

"But maybe if we can hold out long enough, the war will end before they have a chance to kill us."

At that everyone fell silent for a moment, because Erika had expressed the central principle that kept the ghetto going, kept us all in that struggle when it would have been easier to give up. That principle was hope.

"Hope," Rosa said angrily. "Hope is our enemy. We should give up hope, grab their guns, fight, and die proudly."

"Only a person who is full of hope could say such a thing," I said softly.

She turned her head and looked at me. Looked me right in the eye. Again I could feel my face burning.

Then she winked at me and said, "I suppose we all hope for certain things, Daniel, but I don't think you should admit what it is *you* hope for."

Everyone in the room burst out laughing at that. Was it her mission in life to embarrass me? And yet I'd gladly let her do it over and over as long as she was noticing me.

It was moments like that which made you want to stay alive. At any cost.

7

Moments that made you want to stay alive—like the one in this next picture. Erika is sitting with the orchestra, playing her violin. Mother, Father, and I were in the audience, of course, as were Friedrich and Rosa. Rosa and I sat next to each other. My family was so proud of Erika. At thirteen she was the youngest member of the orchestra. It was an evening of Beethoven. I sat beside Rosa, madly in love, and felt the music lift me out of the ghetto, beyond its cruel walls, to a place where the spirit was pure and free. The music reminded me that beauty did exist—somewhere—and suddenly I wanted very much to survive this nightmare. Erika played, as usual, with her soul, and I knew that, to her, music and life were one. After the concert we had a little party at our apartment, with extra bread Mother had managed to bring home and little vegetable patties she fried up out of leftover tops and peelings of the week's vegetables. We all

pretended to enjoy them, although they tasted simply
awful.

I feel the pictures. So few. I had taken only three
rolls of film with me into the ghetto, plus my devel-
oping supplies. I had to be careful, take only the pictures I really wanted. This next one Father insisted on
taking. It was me on my sixteenth birthday, in March
of 1943. I have my arm around Rosa. As usual, she is
smiling.

Rosa was actually from Lodz. Her family had lived
in a beautiful house, had been very well off. Her father
had owned three fur stores. He had been a member of
the Jewish Council that was appointed when the Germans invaded Poland in September of 1939, but in
November most of the leaders were deported, her father among them. That left her mother, an older brother,
Nathan, who was twenty, and a younger brother, Isaac.
By the time the ghetto was sealed off from the rest of
the world, in April 1940, there were 160,500 people
there. By 1943 there were around 80,000 of us left, the
rest having died or been sent away in one of the many
transports.

On my sixteenth birthday Rosa and I went to the little house where the library was hidden. There we met
with our group and on that day made some important
decisions.

Rosa began.

"We all know rumor has it that since the deportations started in 1942, those on the transports have
been going to their deaths. Apparently Mr. Stein found
a letter in a pants pocket when he was sorting through
the clothes sent back from a transport. The letter said
the group had been taken to Chelmno and that they
were to be killed." She paused. "The deportations

have slowed for the moment. But what if they begin again? I think we should be prepared."

"I agree," I added. "We should begin to think of hiding places and set up a warning system so that the group can work together to save people."

Everyone liked the idea. We all felt better thinking that maybe we could *do* something that next time, instead of sitting by helplessly.

And then we had a long discussion about Palestine, a place we all hoped would become a Jewish homeland. We vowed that if we survived we would gather there and become a community. We would work the land and be real pioneers. Some of the group had studied agriculture at school, and they discussed the planting of fruit trees and harvesting of olives. For a moment we were transported out of the ghetto into a magical place of freedom, hard work, and camaraderie.

That summer Rosa and I saw each other every evening. We would meet in the crowded courtyard of our building and try to get the best seats—the ones on the cool brick that surrounded the unused fountain. We would dangle our legs and talk.

"There's a terribly unhappy family living across from us," Rosa told me one night.

"Aren't we all?" I replied.

"No, I don't mean that," she said. "They argue constantly. The father is horrible and greedy. He steals his children's rations. There are two children, a fourteen-year-old boy and a fifteen-year-old girl. The mother must be dead. The children can't stop him from stealing. Of course, they yell and scream and cry, but he doesn't care. They've started to carry their bread with them at all times, because if they leave it out, he'll eat their whole week's ration in one day. But even that doesn't help. He steals from them while they are asleep." She paused. "I'd like to knock his head against the wall!"

I grinned at her. "Why don't you?"

She looked miserable. "He's so much bigger than I am."

"Would you like me to do it?" I was quite tall by then, around five foot eleven, and I would have been strong if I hadn't been so thin.

"Ah," she said with a wink, "a knight in shining armor. The role suits you, Daniel. You were born at the wrong time."

"We were all born at the wrong time," I answered bitterly.

"Well," she said slowly, not willing to argue with me about that, "perhaps we can help those kids without actually having to fight the father."

"How?" I asked.

She thought for a minute. She looked beautiful when she was thinking. I wanted to take her in my arms and kiss her. We rarely got a chance to kiss, though. We were never alone. When there are three, four, five people to a room, where can you find privacy? You can't! Sometimes we could stand in the hallway of her apartment and steal a kiss if no one was coming or going. Still, I was thankful that we had each other. I couldn't believe it when I realized that she liked me too. She had made it quite obvious. One night, after I walked her home, she threw her arms around me and kissed me. I didn't kiss her back because I was so shocked. She teased me about that for weeks. Still, I tried to make up for it.

"Why don't we take his rations one night while he is out at work?" she suggested. "The children also work at night, so he won't be able to accuse them."

"All right," I said, "let's try it."

Two nights later, instead of sitting in the courtyard and talking, Rosa and I made our way to his apartment. We were met there by a friend of Rosa's, a locksmith. He had us inside within a minute. Of course, we didn't know whose rations were whose, but we figured the bread had to be his, as the children carried theirs with them. So we took the bread and left a note:

> *Every time you take food from your*
> *children, we will find a way to take yours.*

We signed it,

> *The Avengers.*

The next night Rosa and I met again.

"Well?" I asked her.

"Oh, the yelling and the screaming was terrible," she reported. "But since he left with the children and returned with them, he knew it couldn't be them. He threatened to go to the police to report the break-in, but the children reminded him that they would have to report *his* thefts then. He accused them of organizing it, but they insisted they knew nothing about it."

A week later Rosa reported that there were no longer fights in the apartment across the way. We had accomplished something.

I made sure that Rosa always had a portion of my extra bread. She worked in a sewing factory that was blazing hot in the summer and freezing cold in the winter and had a terrible kitchen staff, so she ate even less well than we did.

It was that summer of 1943 that Mother began to get ill. It was nothing specific—just one cold or flu or fever after another. She was simply run-down. Still, she knew she couldn't miss work—it was her work at the bakery that kept the rest of us alive, because of the extra bread. So no matter how ill she was, she forced herself to go to work. She became thinner and paler and weaker and couldn't shake her infections. Then winter rolled in on us and it got so cold that the walls had ice on them. We couldn't get enough heat. We had nothing to burn. I started to scavenge. I would go out into empty lots with the other children and try to find old rags, anything that would help the fire burn longer. And then I found a gold mine! Friedrich told me that the apartment beside his had been quiet for some time. We decided to see if everything was all right. A middle-aged man lived alone there then—his wife had died a few months earlier, his children had been taken on one of the transports. No one answered when we knocked. We tried the door and found it unlocked. We went in and found the poor man lying under his thin blanket, frozen to death. I had seen so much death by then, bodies frozen on the street as I walked to work, corpses being loaded into carts to be taken away, that this sight didn't even shock me. In fact, what upset me was that I *wasn't* shocked. Death was familiar now, too familiar.

"Do you want to tell the authorities," Friedrich asked, "or shall I?"

"Neither of us will," I answered. "Not yet."

Friedrich looked at me in surprise. "Why?"

"Look around you, Friedrich, what do you see?"

Friedrich looked around. "Things."

"What things?"

"A table. A bed. A chest of drawers."

"And what are these things made of?"

His eyes lit up. "Wood!"

"We're going to take them apart, piece by piece. You'll take half for your apartment, I'll take half for mine. Mother will die if she has to live in this freezing cold for even one more week. We must do it."

Friedrich didn't object. He knew that the man was dead, that everyone the man loved was dead. The materials would only go to the authorities, who would hand them out to the police and those who ruled over us in the ghetto. Still, if we were caught, we'd be jailed, possibly even hanged. I fetched some of Father's tools, and as quietly as we could, we transferred the materials. Rosa and Erika kept watch for us, because if anyone in the building found out about the apartment it would have been stripped in minutes. Rosa and I managed to smuggle some wood back to her apartment as well. The furniture kept the ice off our walls and kept Mother's illness from turning into pneumonia.

Food supplies became even worse that winter— vegetables became scarce, and on some days we had only bread and soup with a few turnips in it. Erika was nothing but skin and bones. Still, she played her violin every evening, and that seemed to sustain her—she composed her own melodies, beautiful and happy songs that cheered us just listening to them.

"Why should I write sad pieces?" she said. "We're sad enough already."

In March of 1944 it was announced that all musical instruments had to be handed in. Father, once again valuing the soul and how to nurture it, refused to allow Erika to hand hers in. We reported it lost and then hid it in the cupboard along with the radio. She could no longer play, though, and that was terrible for her. After that I noticed a definite decline in her health. I knew that if rescue and the war's end didn't come soon, she and Mother would die, with or without the transports.

8

The next picture is one I took in May 1944. Rosa and Erika stand in front of their sewing factory. I had to take it quickly and when no one was around, as by then owning a camera in the ghetto was illegal. Rosa and Erika made uniforms for German soldiers. I still worked at the metalworks factory where I had been placed in an apprenticeship program. First I'd learned how to strip any machine that came into the workshop, and then I'd learned how to put it back together. Others there made pails or watering cans.

One evening in May, when we were at one of our youth meetings, Rosa began to tell us of the corruption in the soup kitchens at her factory.

"We get a bowl of soup at lunch and an extra one later," she remarked. "There is so little in it that we are just filling up with water. Or it is so disgusting, you can't eat it. What is the soup like at your plant, Daniel?"

"Pretty terrible," I admitted. "But there are potatoes and carrots in it and occasionally a small meat ration."

"You see, I knew it!" she exclaimed. "I'm sure the staff is pilfering the good vegetables and all we get is some turnip tops and potato peels." She paused. I knew that pause well. She was not just daydreaming. She was planning. "Well, I don't think this can go on. I, for one, will refuse to eat it!"

"You'll refuse a meal?" one of the others questioned, astonished. "You can't afford to. You'll get too weak, working all day on an empty stomach."

"I can't afford not to," she replied. "Already many of the workers are unable to carry on—hot water is of no use to us. No, this is the only way."

News had a way of traveling in the ghetto—not by telephone, but by word of mouth. The next morning we heard that the workers at Rosa's sewing factory had refused their soup, and as a result the ringleaders, including Rosa, had been fired. This was really serious. Everyone knew that if you didn't have a job, you would be the first one selected for a transport. Quickly I organized a meeting of the young workers on our floor. I suggested that as a gesture of support we send the workers at the sewing factory soup from *our* kitchens. Solidarity was our only hope. After all, what if the people in our kitchens tried to cheat us? Wouldn't we want the support of workers in other factories? They all agreed, and a few boys and I took the soup over. This really upset the director of the factory, but it gave the workers there a terrific boost. They ate our soup, then declared that they would go on a hunger strike until Rosa and the others were rehired. Later I learned that Erika had organized this plan of action. Erika! Management was furious and wouldn't give in at first. But after two days they rehired Rosa and her friends and established a committee to oversee the kitchen workers and to make sure that all the food that was coming into the factory stayed there.

Rosa was ecstatic.

"You see," she said to Erika and me as we sat in the courtyard together, "we just have to stick together. Daniel, you would have been so proud of Erika. I understand she even gave a speech!"

"Erika, is it true?" I asked. "Did you?"

"A little speech," Erika smiled. "Sometimes a few words is all it takes."

Well, if anyone understood that, Erika did. I gave her a big hug.

"I'm so proud of you," I said.

She actually blushed.

Rosa sighed. "All this struggle," she said, "and for what? I still believe that they'll try to kill us all before the war is over. They're going to lose, we know that now from listening to your radio, but I'm just as sure that they'll kill as many of us as they can before the end. At least that way Hitler will feel he's accomplished something. He may lose the war, but Europe will be free of Jews. I've heard rumors that they're going to destroy the entire ghetto, deport everyone. Daniel, you have to promise me that if anything like that happens, you'll go into hiding. After all, where will they send us? Somewhere better? I don't think so. And what could be worse than this? Only death."

I stared at the ground for a moment before I replied.

"I can't promise," I said quietly. "If my family needs me, I must go with them."

"What good will you be to them dead?" Rosa objected.

But I couldn't give her the promise she asked for. Not with Erika sitting there, thin and pale, with the beginnings of a cough. Perhaps if I went with them, I could help.

Good news and bad came together in the summer of 1944. First Rosa and her family had to move, because the Germans ordered a whole section of the ghetto closed down. It had some of the best apartment buildings in it, and everyone had to find a new place to stay. The bright spot was that we convinced Friedrich to move in with us, the rabbi moved in with another family, and Rosa and her family moved into the first-floor room in our building. It made seeing each other much easier for us.

And then in June we heard the news of D day, the Allied invasion of France, on our radio. We spread the word through the ghetto, and soon everyone was celebrating—right in front of the Germans, too. No one cared. But the Germans were furious. They realized that the only way we could have found out was from radios, and they started to search the ghetto for them. A number of people were arrested. They never even searched our apartment. We were lucky. But we were *very* careful from then on to listen only when we were sure no one was around who could inform on us. That was a wonderful day. Still, Rosa was convinced that our doom was still sealed. Erika was sure we would be saved. I wavered between hope and despair. In July we heard that a coup against Hitler had failed. We were devastated, but it did give us hope to realize that some Germans were turning against their great leader. The Russians were advancing. But was it fast enough? Because just as Rosa had predicted, the Germans ordered more mass transports out of the ghetto.

Postmen ran from house to house, delivering the "wedding invitations"—that's what we called the orders. Everyone lived in fear. Our youth group went to work, hiding those notified. Some people ran for days from house to apartment to cellar but finally gave up, too tired and hungry to run and hide anymore. The Germans reduced the size of the ghetto to only four blocks, so it was hard to find anywhere to hide. And then in August our notice came....

Mother was very sick by then. She had tuberculosis. She'd had to leave her job a few weeks earlier because she could pass the disease on to others. Erika had also developed a terrible cough. The doctor said it was bronchitis. She needed medicine, but there was none. She ran a fever, had chills, coughed violently.

When the final transports were announced in August, most Jews refused to go—they stayed home instead of reporting to the train station. Then Hans Biebow, the German in charge of the ghetto, made a speech to the Jews. He told us that we were being sent into Germany to work for the war effort. He said that when the Russians came, they would deal with us harshly because we had worked for the Germans. And some people fell for it. They believed him!

The Russians were so close, but couldn't they move faster? I was in a fever pitch of dread and expectation.

Father called a meeting.

"I have been thinking of our alternatives," he said. "Mother and Erika are very weak because of their illnesses. The only place I've found where we could all hide is a cellar underneath the bakery. It's very damp and cold, and I'm afraid that a few days down there would mean death for them. Therefore we will go on the transport and hope that we are being sent to another work camp. But not you, Daniel. Or you, Friedrich."

"I want to go with you," I objected.

"No. The Russians will be here soon. They will not punish us, as Biebow says. We all know that. They will liberate us. And you will be here when they do. Wait until after we leave, when it is dark and no one can see where you're going. Then sneak over to the bakery. Grab some bread on your way down to the cellar."

That night Erika, Rosa, and I had our last meeting in the courtyard. Friedrich couldn't be there, as he was working a night shift.

I felt terrible about my family leaving without me. I was sure I would never see them again.

"If I had the power of God," I said bitterly, "I would wipe the entire human race off the face of the earth. It's a complete failure. Look around us, a race of monsters."

And then Erika yelled at me.

"Don't you ever say that, Daniel!" she said. "I'm ashamed of you."

I was so stunned, I couldn't reply. But Rosa came to my defense.

"Erika, what's wrong with you? Daniel's right. How can you look around you, see most of the people you loved murdered and tortured, and think anything else? How could these things happen if the world were a decent place?"

"Rosa," Erika replied, "I'm ashamed of you, too. Don't you see? This is the way the Nazis think. They believed that we Jews weren't good enough to live, and so they decided to wipe us off the face of the earth. Who were they to decide who should live and who should die? And who are you?"

For once Rosa didn't have an answer, and neither did I.

"We are alive. We are human, with good and bad in us. That's all we know for sure. We can't create a new species or a new world. That's been done. Now we have to live within those boundaries. What are our choices? We can despair and curse, and change nothing. We can choose evil like our enemies have done and create a world based on hate. Or we can try to make things better.

"Why have we fought so hard to survive all these years? So we could go to our deaths in despair? We must live, and when this is all over, we must work to make the world a better place." Then she paused. "And if we die, we will die knowing that it was not our fault, that we did our best, and we can go to our deaths in dignity. You're both strong. I want you both to live. And to start over in Palestine. And to have children. And to remember those of us who were destroyed by the worst in humanity, by its hate." She paused again. "You must choose love. Always choose love."

Rosa and I were both crying by the time Erika finished speaking. We hugged her and held on tight to her and I knew she was right. My little sister. Tears flow down my face as I think of it now. Timid, silent Erika, who turned out to be the bravest, most eloquent of us all.

9

That same night Rosa and I said our good-byes in the corridor outside her flat. "I'm not going to tell you where I'm hiding, Daniel," she said. "That way, if you are caught, there's no chance of you giving me away. But don't worry. It's *very* safe. I wish you could come with me and hide there. But there isn't room for both you and Friedrich.

"Our whole family is going to hide," she added. "Even Mama. She is sure the transports are going to a place called Auschwitz—a camp built for killing people. A death camp. That's what she hears from those who load and clean the trains."

"It'll soon be over, Rosa. If we make it through, how will we find each other?"

"We'll meet each other here, Daniel, in Lodz. I'll leave you a note in your old apartment, telling you where we are living."

She threw her arms around me.

"Daniel, you must live. Don't let them defeat you. Erika is right. We must try."

"I'll try," I promised. "I'll try."

And then we kissed. I didn't want to let her go. I held on to her for dear life and she to me.

The door to her apartment opened.

"Rosa," her older brother said, "it's time to go." He shook my hand. "Good luck, Daniel."

"You too, Nathan," I managed to get out, and then I turned and, without looking back, ran up the stairs to our apartment.

The next morning Father, Mother, and Erika packed their clothes and left for the train station. First they hugged Friedrich good-bye. Then Mother held my face between her hands and stared at me with tears in her eyes. I too took a long last look at her. We knew we might never see each other again. "God bless you and keep you," she said. I kissed her and Erika and Father.

"I love you," Erika said to me.

"I love you too."

"Be strong, Daniel," Father said. "Be strong."

"I will, Father."

We hugged. And they left. We were alone.

All that day we sat quietly in my room, not daring to make a sound. Finally night came.

"I think we should go one at a time," said Friedrich. "Less likely to draw attention to ourselves. And if they catch us—only one will get caught."

I nodded. "Who goes first?"

"Let me," Friedrich said. "If you see any trouble, don't follow."

"No," I said, "let me."

But Friedrich was suddenly out the door. "See you there!" he called back.

I watched him from the window as he moved down the street, going from door to door. Finally he disappeared from sight. I left the window and checked the cupboard. All my valuables were there—most of my pictures (I'd kept a few in my boot), my diary, my camera, Erika's violin, the radio, and my copy of *The Count of Monte Cristo*. The bed was in front of it, the comforter on. I took one last look out the window and then opened the door. The corridor was empty. I crept down the stairs and paused before opening the door to the street. I heard no noise, no footsteps, and felt it was probably safe. I slipped through the door and darted for the next doorway.

"Halt!"

My heart started to pound and I broke out in a cold sweat. In a split second I had to decide whether to stop or make a run for the shadows.

"Halt or I'll shoot." The words were German. I stopped.

In a moment two Gestapo guards were behind me, a gun pressed into my back.

"Move! Hurry up."

I ended up being shoved into this freight car—one of the last to be loaded. I didn't see Friedrich. Maybe he made it. Perhaps Father and Mother and Erika are on the same train. Often it takes a full day and part of the night to load them full of people. I resolved to be strong, as Father said. Whatever is in store, I shall try to meet it bravely.

The sun is up now. I tuck the pictures back into my boot, where I'd kept them—just in case I was captured. Erika was right. There was so much that was good in those pictures. I must try to concentrate on that, not on the overwhelming evil of the Nazis. They will not defeat me if I can help it—not if I can help it.

The train slows down and finally comes to a jarring stop. The doors are thrown open and we are ordered out. Prisoners dressed in striped pajamas help us out of the car. Many in the car are dead. I look around, desperately trying to catch a glimpse of my family. People from other cars aren't treated as politely. "Out! Out!" German guards scream. There are many guards with machine guns and dogs. There is panic everywhere as people scream and call to family members. We are pushed toward an enclosure, where we are told to leave all our belongings. I put down my rucksack, but I leave the pictures in my boot. I think of the rest of the pictures hidden in the cupboard along with my diary. Maybe if I don't survive, some-one will find it all. And remember me. We are hur-ried out of the enclosure and marched back along the railroad tracks.

We reach a huge open field. Barracks are on eith-er side of the field, and to our left there are chimneys. Smoke pours out of the chimneys, and the glow hov-ers over the camp. There is a terrible smell from the smoke, which makes me gag. I have never smelled anything like it. The field is full of people who must've arrived from all over Europe, many with the Star of David sewn to their coats or jackets.

Desperately I look for my family—and then I see them! They are a few hundred yards ahead of me. I scream, "Mother, Father, Erika!" But they can't hear me, because suddenly a selection has begun. Dogs bark, soldiers scream, the men are beaten about the head and back. Lines are being formed. Women on the right, men on the left, all in single file. Then the

SS officers go through the women's line and separate some of the healthier-looking women from the children and old women. The children scream and cry, the mothers try to run after them. Some are beaten, one is shot. Both lines are marched off. I push my way through the crowd of men until I am behind Father.

"Father!"

He turns. His face shows only disappointment.

"They caught you!" he says, tears coming to his eyes.

"It's all right, Father. We'll go through this together," I say. "Together we'll be stronger."

He hugs me close.

And then our selection begins. A German stands at the front of the line and points with his thumb to the right or to the left. One side will live, one will die. That much I know.

"Slap your cheeks, Father," I order. "Bite your lips." He does so. "Stand up straight."

Father is only forty years old. He looks much older because of everything we've been through. Still, he isn't sick and his hair is black. That should help. I bite my lips and pinch my cheeks. The line moves slowly. I can see that those being sent to the right are old and sick looking. It is my father's turn. He is sent to the left. And then it is my turn. I too am sent to the left.

We are taken into a barracks, where we are forced to undress. We have to leave our things. I tuck my pictures deep into my boots. Then we are hustled into a long room that has two benches running down the center, and prisoners with razors standing along the benches. The guards are constantly screaming at us and pushing us, so we don't have time to think or react. Our heads are shaved, and then our entire bodies. The barbers cut us as they shave us. Then the guards push us into another room, where prisoners pour disinfectant over us. I can't help but scream. It is terribly painful, because I am bleeding from the cuts the barbers gave me. I shut my eyes and put my hands over them so none of the disinfectant gets into my eyes. Everyone is screaming. We're rushed into another room, where striped uniforms and wooden clogs are thrown at us, and then we are beaten and pushed outside and into another building. We dress as we run. I can't find Father. I know he must be here, but I can't find him. And I realize that I will never see my pictures again. God, how I hate them for taking everything away from me!

Finally we are pushed into a large barracks where there are three tiers of bunks.

"Father, Father," I cry.

A man in front of me turns around.

"Daniel?"

"Father?"

We are so changed, with our shaved heads and uniforms, we didn't even recognize each other.

"It suits you, Father," I say, trying to smile.

He grabs me and hugs me.

"Mother and Erika are dead, Daniel. I found out from a guard that the smoke is from bodies burning. But first they are taken into huge rooms and then gas is thrown in and they choke to death. Oh, God help us. All that suffering and then to die like that."

"Father, they may have survived the selection," I whisper. "We did."

"Into your bunks!" a German guard yells as he

swats at Father with his stick. "Now!"

Father and I scramble into a bunk with ten others. Lights are turned out. The only sounds are the moans and sighs of men and boys like us, who have just lost everything.

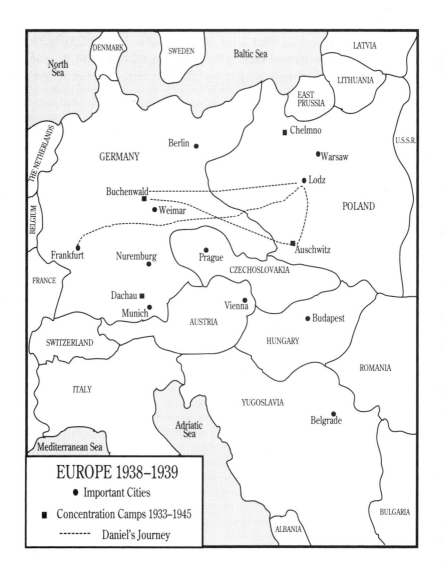

PART THREE

PICTURES OF AUSCHWITZ

10

Father sits with his legs astride me, holding on to me as if we were on a toboggan run. I hold on to the man in front of me the same way. We are in an open boxcar, traveling by train. It is night. It is snowing. The wind is fierce, but the man in front of me is a large Pole, and I am quite protected. Father is not so lucky—I am too skinny to give him much protection from the elements. We were loaded onto these cars today after three months in Auschwitz/Birkenau and a long march away from the death camp. It is the middle of December.

I slept most of the day. But now the cold and the terrible hunger keep me awake. We've had nothing to eat but a slice of bread and a cup of watery soup this morning. The Allies are advancing. The Russians are nearing Auschwitz, and the Germans are starting to evacuate the camp. We are being taken back to Germany, I suppose so they can continue to use us for forced labor and, of course, to kill us. They want to kill us not only because they hate and despise us but also now because they want no one left to tell the world what happened. Then they can't be punished. But why do they think they'll be punished? After all, don't they believe that what they are doing is right? They are just eradicating a vile species—like cockroaches. Surely no one would punish them for that. But no, they are terrified. Does that mean they knew all along it was wrong—and they did it anyway, some for the love of killing and for the love of power, some because they were simply following orders, orders with which they agreed?

I am more determined than ever to live. I will live and I will bear witness against them. I will remember.

I don't have my pictures anymore. Still, I can make pictures in my head. I will do that. And I will go over them now and organize these pictures so that when the time comes to tell of what happened, I will tell it clearly. They will not defeat me. I hug Father's arms closer around my chest. And I will *not* let them defeat Father, either. I will keep him alive with the last ounce of strength in my body. I have spent two train trips looking at pictures, and I will do the same on this one—even if all I have are the pictures in my head. I remember how confused I was on that first trip, how terrified on the second. Now I am simply a ball of anger and fury and determination. If I die, it won't be without a fight.

Everything is in pictures for me now, as if I were clicking with my camera every time I saw something. The most memorable picture of those months is the one of Erika. Father was convinced that she and Mother had gone straight to the gas chambers. I kept telling him that we couldn't be sure. For four weeks we were kept in quarantine. We were actually in the part of the camp called Birkenau. Auschwitz had three major camps—Auschwitz I; Auschwitz II, or Birkenau; and Auschwitz III, or Monowitz.

Auschwitz I was the main camp. It was built of red-brick buildings and housed much of the camp administration, plus some barracks for political prisoners of many nationalities. Birkenau had the gas chambers and crematoria. After you entered the gate, on the left was the women's camp. On the right were the men's camp, the quarantine camp, the Theresienstadt family camp, the Gypsy camp, and the prisoners' hospital. Behind all of this was "Canada," as we called it, a group of storehouses containing all the loot stolen from prisoners as they arrived: mountains of shoes, coats, clothes, shaving brushes, even artificial limbs, all to be sorted and shipped back to Germany. Monowitz was a labor camp where German firms forced inmates to work in synthetic-oil and rubber factories.

Every barracks had a kapo in charge—a prisoner, often a criminal, sometimes a Jew. Father made sure that the kapo in charge of us knew of my skills with machinery and his skills as a carpenter and jack-of-all-trades. When quarantine was over, some men were sent to build more barracks in Birkenau. The Nazis were so deluded, many still believed they could win, and then of course they'd need more room for Hitler's enemies from all over Europe. Father and I were sent to Monowitz to work in one of the factories there. Because, you see, even as they were building more barracks for prisoners, they were dismantling the machinery at the factories and sending it back to Germany so the Russians wouldn't capture it. They weren't thinking straight at all, but what could you expect from them? I suppose the businessmen at the factories knew the true story and were anxious to save their precious machines. These men and their businesses thrived on slave labor just as the pharaohs had in Egypt when they used Jewish slaves to build their pyramids. Still, even the pharaohs hadn't attempted the destruction of an entire people.

One of the first things you noticed in Auschwitz was the music. Bands of inmates were forced to play outside, as prisoners were marched to work or to their deaths. There was always music. Happy marching songs, waltzes. Still, this music didn't inspire. This music mocked.

Father and I were put in a barracks with 800 other men. Three of us had to share one straw pallet. There wasn't room even to turn over.

Quarantine had been a nightmare. We lay together all night on the cold floor, not an inch between bodies. At four thirty A.M. they would beat us and kick us out into the freezing cold of the field outside. There we would stand, sometimes for three or four hours, until every single person, not just in our barracks but in the entire camp, was counted. If you fell or tripped, you were whipped or shot. They had to make sure that not *one* inmate would escape the fate planned for him by the Germans. Not one. No one was allowed inside during the day. The sun blazed down on us and we were desperate for water, but there was none to drink—only the midday soup, which was almost all water. We didn't even have our own bowls or spoons to eat with. Five of us would have to share a bowl of soup, passing it from person to person, one sip for each, until it was finished.

Conditions in the new barracks were little better. We were given a ration of bread and margarine and a teaspoon of jam every few days. But we had a brutal kapo who beat and terrorized us at every opportunity. Father and I had to march four miles to work every morning. And when we marched, the band would play. Of course, you were not to look at anything as you marched or you'd be beaten, but that first morning something made me look up at the band, which sat slightly back from the road. And there she was. Little Erika. Playing a violin.

She looked pale and almost like a skeleton, and I could see she was coughing. I could also see that she'd given up. Her eyes were hollow, empty. She thought we were dead, I knew it. Before I could think of what to do, we were past her. Father was marching behind me, and I dared not turn around to tell him. When we got to the factory at Monowitz, we were separated.

I was put to work in the large rubber factory, dismantling equipment. Working in the place was like a nightmare. The factories in Lodz seemed like heaven in comparison. Workers were beaten, whipped, or shot for not performing up to standard. SS men screamed, swore, shouted—it was chaotic and wild. And in the midst of all this, men in pressed brown business suits walked, stepping over dead bodies as if they were rags, checking with the foremen on progress, and giving directions.

Mostly Hungarian Jews made up my work squad. We couldn't understand each other, but it really didn't matter. My mind was on doing my work so I wouldn't get into trouble. And figuring out a way to see Erika. She hadn't noticed me, I was sure of that. I'd have to get her attention without attracting that of the guards.

It was strange. Frankfurt after the Nazis took over had seemed like a nightmare compared to the way it had been before. And Lodz had seemed like a nightmare compared to Frankfurt. And now every minute in this hell, looking at the chimneys constantly belching smoke and fire, knowing that people like myself, children, mothers, were going up in flames, this was worse than anything I could imagine. Was there more? Could it get worse? I didn't think so. What could be worse than mass murder? But I was afraid that I had not yet hit bottom. I was afraid that the Nazis could prove to me that even this was not the worst.

If only I could write Erika a note, I thought. But I had no paper, and if you were caught stealing the least thing, you would be shot. Then I had an idea. I went to the kapo in charge of our unit and asked for a rag to oil down the machine I was working on. He found me one, and a small vial of oil. When he wasn't looking, I bit into the cloth and ripped it in half—it was filthy and disgusting and I had to spit many times to clean my mouth out. Then I dipped my finger into some black grease from the machine I was working on. I wrote on the cloth D&F ALIVE. That's all I had room for. Then I had to figure out how to hide it. Our striped pajamas had no pockets—after all, what would we own that would call for pockets? We had nothing. Still, my pants were held up by string because they were too wide. I tucked the cloth into the string at my waist. The day dragged by. For lunch we were served soup made out of nettles—how did they imagine we could continue to work for them with that kind of ration? But I suppose they didn't care. There were plenty more of us slaves, and when we got too weak, we'd be sent to the gas chambers and someone else would take our place.

Finally it was time to march back. I rejoined the group from our barracks, and we marched five abreast. I managed to get myself on the end of the line, with Father beside me. Until I saw him, I hadn't realized how uncomfortable I'd been with him gone. He was everything to me now, and I didn't like to be separated from him for a minute.

"Father," I said as we marched. "Father, I saw Erika."

He almost stopped. He stumbled. I grabbed him and kept him moving so our SS guard wouldn't notice.

"Are you sure?"

"She was playing in the band as we marched out. She doesn't look good, but she's alive! I've written her a note. I'm going to try to get it to her as we march by."

"They kill you here for less than that, Daniel. Be careful."

"I will."

We marched on in silence. Still, how could I get it to her without the SS guard's noticing?

Slowly I took it out and began to fold it as we walked. I folded it carefully into smaller and tighter squares, until it was only a tiny ball. We had been working since six A.M. It was now six P.M. and we were being forced to march in step four miles back to camp. But I didn't feel it. For once I wasn't tired. I wasn't hungry. I just thought about Erika. My heart pounded. I broke out in a sweat. I could hear the band. We got closer. And there she was, in the second row, second from the end, playing. I waited until I was about two feet away, and then, with a flick of my wrist, I lobbed my missile. It hit her on the elbow. She looked up, puzzled, but dared not stop playing. I could see her eyes searching, and then we were past her. I swore at myself. It was stupid. She'd probably just think it was a piece of garbage.

"I saw her!" Father exclaimed. And then he started to weep. "Thank God. Do you think Mother, too, could be . . . ?"

"Father," I said gently, trying to fight back my tears, trying to be strong for him as he had always been for me, "you know how sick Mother was."

"Yes, yes, I know," he said. The sick, the children, the old, they were first for the ovens, because they couldn't work.

And he continued to weep, for Mother but also with relief that Erika was still alive.

11

The next morning as we marched by, I could see Erika scanning the crowd. I had made sure that I was on the side nearest her. And then her eyes lit on me. And that is the picture of little Erika I will always remember. She continued to play, but her face broke out into a smile, and as I marched past, also smiling, she played a few extra notes just for me. Then she saw Father, and I saw the tears spill from her eyes. She never stopped playing. But in her eyes there was hope now instead of emptiness and death. That was when I knew for certain that Mother was dead. Had Mother been alive, Erika would not have let herself sink into such despair. She must have believed she was the only one of us left. I wondered where she was staying and how I could get to see her.

The train rattles on. It is dead of night now, and cold. I think of the next picture. I don't want to think about it. But I must. It is the worst thing I have ever seen—beyond nightmare, beyond belief. It is of bodies burning in pits, because the crematoria weren't eliminating the bodies as quickly as the Nazis were gassing them. So they threw them into huge pits.

I'd been slaving at the factory for about a week when a new worker was added to my group. It was Adam, a boy from our youth group in Lodz. I was delighted to see him. He was a big fellow, a Polish Jew who spoke Yiddish. On our lunch break he motioned me over to him, and we sat slightly away from the others, our backs against a stack of wood. He spoke in a low voice.

"Don't give up, Daniel. The Russians are close. And there's a resistance here. I'm part of it. I think you should be too. In fact, there's something very important that needs doing, and I think you're just the right person for the job."

"Whatever it is, I'll do it," I declared. "Anything is better than sitting here like a helpless rabbit."

"Right," he said. "I'll see what can be done."

The next day he told me more.

"Hundreds of thousands of Hungarian Jews are being transported here, all to be gassed. Already some in the resistance have smuggled out people and a couple of photos to the outside. But we need more evidence. We must convince them that with a few bombs the gas chambers could be destroyed. And the Germans can't kill us at this rate—I'm told it's almost twenty-five thousand a day—without the gas chambers. There are a ton of cameras in Canada." (The storehouse complex was called Canada because it was bountiful and full of good things, just like the country the prisoners had named it after.) "I've told my contacts about your camera in the ghetto—how you took pictures all those years without getting caught. They want you to take some pictures. Of the gas chambers, if we can manage it. Otherwise of the fire pits where they're burning the bodies."

A chill ran through me. I realized at once how dangerous this would be. And if something happened to me, who would look after Father?

"I'd like to think about it," I replied.

"Not for too long," Adam cautioned. "We'll have to do lots of planning."

Once back in the barracks I had to try to decide whether to tell Father or not. We were able to sneak a look at Erika twice a day then, and that morning Father had gotten away with tossing her a small ration of bread, first making sure the guard wasn't looking. I knew he wouldn't want me to take any chances. Still, I felt I owed it to him to tell him—in case I didn't come back from the mission. There was no privacy in the barracks, nowhere even to crouch, so we squatted just outside the building.

"There's a resistance movement here," I told him. "And they know I'm a photographer. They want me to take some pictures. They'll smuggle them out in the hope they can convince the Allies that mass murders are actually taking place."

For a moment he didn't reply. When he did, his response shocked me.

"You must do it, Daniel, if you want to. We are all just waiting to be sent to the gas chambers. They'll kill us one way or another. Maybe you can help stop it."

"I'll try."

"But you must let me help. I've got some contacts. I can make things in the factory and exchange them for things you could find useful, like a case to conceal the camera. And an I.D. that would show you to be a laborer who works in the Canada complex, or a kapo—someone who might legitimately have to be where you're going. Maybe even a new uniform."

The next day I told Adam I'd do it. The first thing they had to figure out was how to get me out of the work detail so I could be where I had to be. For a week I heard nothing from them. Then one day Adam sat me down and explained the plan.

"We'll do it on one of your days off," he explained. We were given one day off every two weeks. "On that day a kapo from the barracks being built will ask for you and your father and about ten others to come on a work detail. The pits for burning bodies are through the woods parallel to the new barracks. You'll be given the camera at the barracks. You and three others will be ordered to carry some supplies from the building site to the pits. The SS guards at the pits will be told you're delivering it to help the burning. Somehow you'll have to take your pictures. Then you'll be marched to Canada, because we want to get some pictures there of the mountains of goods—it should give the Allies some idea of what we're talking about. Especially helpful would be to get a picture of the hair. The women's hair is packaged and sent back to Germany. A picture of a mountain of hair in bags would be very useful."

Adam spoke of these horrors in the most matter-of-fact way.

"You talk of it so calmly," I commented with a shudder.

And then he gave me a look I will never forget. I can't even describe it well. Only my camera could have captured it. It was a look that said "I have seen more pain than I can deal with, don't ask anything of me, I cannot give it."

"When we arrived on the transport," Adam said to me, "I had my little sister Anya by the hand. They tore her from me and one SS man threw her over to another. She screamed for me, 'Adam, Adam.' Then the SS man took her little body so she was faceup looking at him, and he raised his knee and broke her back, like it was a stick. Then he threw her away onto the ground. I live only for revenge now," he added before he moved away.

By the time the next free day came, I was in a general state of terrible anxiety mixed with excitement. For once I was going to be able to *do* something. My father also seemed in better spirits. By then he had managed to develop quite a secret trade. He manufactured spoons and knives at the foundry where he worked. It was dangerous, but he felt it was worth the risk. He bartered the utensils for two bowls, one for each of us, a nicely made cloth case that attached to my string belt under my top, to hold the camera, and a new uniform so I could pass for a worker from the Canada complex, because they always looked clean and neat. We kissed each other that morning at the four thirty roll call and he wished me luck. At five A.M. orders came for our departure.

A kapo I had never seen took charge of us. He beat a few of us around the head and he kicked Father savagely. I wondered if the plan was still on—surely this couldn't be a resistance man. And if it was, I thought he played his part a bit too convincingly. It was not a long march from our barracks to the building site. We were given the job of lugging huge slabs of wood that sat in a large pile over to a barracks in progress. The slabs were heavy and it took two people to carry one. It was terrible work. Soon the skin over my shoulder bone was cut and bleeding as the wood pressed down relentlessly. As Father and I were lowering a slab, the kapo came up to me and punched me in the stomach. I doubled over. The kapo reached down as if to give me another blow, but instead he slipped me the camera.

Clutching my stomach, I quickly tucked it into its case and muttered to the kapo, "Have you ever heard of pretending?" Surely his blows didn't have to be so real!

We continued to work until mid-morning, when he ordered three pairs of us to follow him into the woods. He then pointed out three vats of alcohol that had been left under the trees. We picked them up and followed him to the clearing. Smoke seared our faces, and the stench of burnt flesh was so horrible, I thought I'd faint. He marched up to one of the SS guards on duty and informed him that we had been ordered to pour extra alcohol over the fire, as it wasn't burning fast enough. The guard nodded and let us proceed. We threw the alcohol onto the blaze, and for one terrible moment I was forced to look into the pit.

There I saw corpses of every size turning black from heat. And I realized that people I knew could be in there, that they were not just bodies but each one a murdered human being. And I almost threw myself in with them. That was the closest I'd come to ending it all, which was strange, because it was supposed to be the moment I defied the Nazis and could once again feel like a human being. But what did it mean to be a human being? That we could do this to our brothers and sisters? Perhaps it would be better to resign from the human race altogether. It was my father who saved me. He came up behind me and spoke quietly.

"Daniel, if we let them kill all those who still

remember what it is to be human, what will be left?"

Still, I wasn't convinced. I didn't care.

"Daniel, if you jump, I'll jump after you."

I knew he meant it. I couldn't be responsible for his death. I took the camera out of its case and made sure the exposure was such that the flames would look like a bright white background and the blackened bodies would show through clearly. I took three pictures before I put the camera back. Then I threw the rest of the alcohol into the pit and turned away, the blistering heat tearing through me.

Our kapo then marched us toward the Canada complex. To get there, we had to pass rows of people just off the transports and on their way to the gas chambers. I looked at all of them, women, children, old men, even healthy men, and I wanted to warn them that soon they'd be nothing but ashes. But I knew I'd be killed on the spot. So many SS, so many dogs surrounded them. And if any Canadian told them of their fate, the Canadian was thrown live into the crematoria fires. After all, destruction on such a huge scale demanded that the victims know nothing. Even now an SS officer was calling out, "Hurry, please. You'll be disinfected and have showers, and then you'll be reunited with your families in the camp. Make sure you fold your clothes neatly. Remember where they are so you can retrieve them after your showers. Hurry now, please."

How could they imagine, these Jews from Hungary, what was in store for them? In fact, I believe it was only those of us who had been held in Poland who suspected the real truth. How could the others even imagine it?

We were marched to Canada, where we returned

the empty alcohol vats. With great authority the kapo marched us into various storehouses. I managed to take three more pictures; any more would have been too dangerous. On the way back to the building site, I handed the camera over to the kapo. He tucked it into his inside jacket pocket. As he did so, he gave me a wink. And then a kick. The wink wasn't much, but it lifted my spirits enormously. We'd pulled it off! I just prayed that they could get the photos out of the camp and into the hands of someone who could do something.

Even now the fiery image of that day stays burned in my mind—I will never, ever forget it.

12

I see Adam, fire in his eyes, determined. There he is again, blood slowly oozing from his wounds.

It was only days after our picture-taking that Adam hinted to me that the resistance was on the move. "We're planning something very big," he told me one morning. "Men have escaped to the Allies and told them of the gas chambers, and still they do nothing. Your photos may arrive too late to save this last batch of Jews—although you'll be glad to know that the fellow who escaped with them still hasn't been captured."

The next morning SS men on motorcycles roared up to the factories we were working in. Everyone was ordered back to the barracks, because Crematorium IV was burning. It had been blown up—sabotaged. We marched back, heads held high.

Later that day we heard that most of the rebels had been killed—but not before killing a few SS guards first. That day they gave us our rations when we got back to the barracks—unheard of, really. After all, if someone should die before night, then those rations he'd eaten would be wasted. That was why rations were given only *after* a full day's work. They must have been very upset to forget that rule. I ate my quarter loaf of bread slowly throughout the day, not all at once, as I usually did. And Father had some time for extra bartering.

Father and I had quickly learned that if you simply ate your rations, worked, and followed orders, your life span would be a few months at the most. You would grow so thin and wasted that you would be chosen for the gas chamber in the regular selections the Nazis made. Father made sure that he kept up a brisk trade in the spoons and knives he made at the factory. New arrivals would trade him a slice of bread or something else he felt we needed. Sometimes he managed to get us potatoes, sometimes a bit of sausage, even some cheese. (We were given two ounces of sausage three times a week and two ounces of cheese on Sunday, and people would trade it if need be.) Knives for cutting bread were very much in demand, as were spoons for the soup. Though only on Sunday did the soup have anything of substance in it; on other days it was brewed from weeds and thistles. Father kept us from becoming so weak and emaciated that we couldn't continue.

The following day we were sent back to work as usual, the uprising easily contained by the SS. Our group was ordered to carry boxes of supplies from the yard to the factory. When we were out in the yard, Adam whispered to me, "All the others have been captured. They'll give me away under torture. I don't want to be caught and tortured. I won't give them the satisfaction. I'll have my revenge."

I whispered back, "Adam, your revenge will be seeing

them defeated. It can't be long now. They may not discover you. Don't do it."

"I've made up my mind," he answered. "Good luck to you, Daniel. Remember me. And now stay away from me."

I could see that he would not change his mind, so I quickly moved away, toward some crates. An SS man stood directing the unloading, his back to Adam. Adam moved up on him quickly, quietly, and pulled the guard's pistol from its holster before the guard could stop him. He shot the SS man at point-blank range, then turned around and fired at two more guards who were close by. He wounded one; the other killed Adam with a hail of machine-gun fire. I crouched behind the crates, only too aware of the wild hatred this would instill in the SS guards. They would cheerfully massacre all of us in revenge. But no, for the moment they seemed occupied in getting medical help for the wounded guard who was still alive. In the meantime the rest of our group slipped back into the factory and to our jobs. I couldn't stop my hands from trembling as I worked. I knew that as punishment they might well take Adam's work squad, line us up, and shoot us all. Or hang us publicly to make an example of us. There were often bodies hanging from the gallows as we marched to work. Still, I wasn't angry at Adam. I admired him. He had chosen his way to die. I took a deep breath. If the rest of us had to die for that act, then so be it. I stopped trembling. And I vowed that if they came for us, I would be shot fighting too.

But no one came and our day continued as usual. That night as we marched back to our barracks, I resolved to see Erika. Passing her twice a day and not being allowed to talk was unbearable. So the next day I again made a note out of cloth and grease. It said FENCE, and I lobbed it at her as we went by at the end of the day. This time I saw her bend over and pick it up, pretending she had dropped her violin bow. After we had been given our rations, Father and I headed for the electrified barbed-wire fence that separated the men's camp from the women's. We had to walk past ten barracks, but finally we reached the fence. And there she was. We dared not get too close for fear of getting in trouble with the guards. But we called to each other.

"I love you," Father called.

"I love you too," she cried back.

"Mother?" Father asked.

She shook her head.

"I won't make the next selection," she called. "But you two must. Also we might be moved. There's a rumor."

"If you're moved, you won't have to go through the selection," I called. "Perhaps it'll be for the best. Try, Erika. Try."

A kapo from the barracks near where Erika stood rushed toward her.

"Get away from there, you whore!" she screamed, swinging her club.

Erika was fast. She moved too quickly for the blows to strike. But then she was gone. And Father and I melted back into the crowd of men at the barracks, not wanting to attract the attention of the guards.

In my mind I can see Erika. "Try," I had called to her. She was so thin, she couldn't have weighed more than fifty pounds. But her face had that particular spiritual glow that I knew so well, which had died for a while when she thought she was alone. Now just knowing we were alive had helped her. The next day her spot was filled by someone else. My heart sank. Neither Father nor I knew what it meant. Had she been sent to the gas chambers? Or moved out of the camp?

That night I lay in my bunk, teeth chattering, head bursting with pain. I felt terrible. I was burning hot one minute, freezing cold the next. I had typhus. Father bribed the kapo to let me stay in the barracks while I was sick. We all knew that being sent to the infirmary was usually a death sentence, because Nazi doctors were trained not to heal but to select those too weak to work for death. I was delirious and in a fever for five days.

Avoiding typhus was very difficult because we lived in the most horrific squalor. Our blankets crawled with so many lice that it often seemed like the blankets themselves were alive—they moved. We were allowed to wash once a day in a trickle of water, but the toilets were just long slabs of wood with holes in them and they were always filthy and overflowing. We deloused and cleaned ourselves on our day off every other Sunday, but it made little difference. Still, I was lucky that Father had things the kapo wanted. He took me off the work detail and allowed me to lie alone in the barracks all day.

I dreamed of Mother in my delirium. It was strange. I had been so busy trying to stay alive I'd had no time to mourn her death. But those five days were filled with her image. She scolded me for not wearing my overcoat when I was cold, she nagged me to eat some more coffee cake or noodle pudding. I had forgotten those things existed. She hugged me to her and told me she loved me. When I came out of my delirium and told Father, he said that she had been with me every moment of my illness and that she had pulled me through.

"Her memory?" I asked him.

"No, Daniel, her spirit. She was with you. I just know it. I could feel her sometimes late at night when you were crying out. She would soothe you and you would quiet down."

I didn't know what to make of what Father said. He had never been religious; I don't think he used to believe in God. But if he felt Mother's presence, he must have believed in something. Why would this experience, which should make any sane person *not* believe in God, do the opposite to him?

And yet somehow I felt he was right. I didn't know how I felt about God—after all, how could He let us suffer so? Still, somewhere inside me I *knew* Mother had been with me. I came through my illness very weak, but feeling more at peace with myself than I had before. Perhaps Erika was right. We were here, and to despair was useless. And then I thought of Rosa. Thoughts of her washed over me in such a rush of pain and longing, I could barely stand it. As I'd done with Mother, I had tried to put her out of my head. But from then on they both stayed with me as a reminder of good and as a reminder that love still existed, even here.

And then, about six weeks later, near the end of November, our kapo rushed into the barracks, screaming, "Out, out!" We were counted and marched out of the camp. The Russians were nearing. Before we left, the Nazis dynamited the gas chambers and the crematoria so that no evidence of them would survive.

They gave us a quarter loaf of bread the day we marched out of Auschwitz, and that was all we ate for three days. At first we marched five in a row, but quickly the line began to thin out, and it became apparent to the Germans that this was another way to kill even more of us. As soon as a prisoner fell, either from exhaustion or simply because he had tripped, he was shot. Bodies were strewn along the road.

I realized that this march would kill most of us, that the escape from the gas chambers was not necessarily an escape from brutal death.

"We must concentrate on only one thing," I said to Father. "Putting one foot carefully in front of the other. Watch where you step. Don't allow yourself even to stumble."

And that is what we did. Soon those who were too weak to walk begged for help and everyone who could ended up supporting one other. I supported a boy just a year younger than I, who turned out to be from Lodz. His name was Peter. Of course I asked him if he'd known Rosa, but he hadn't. From the moment we began to talk, we liked each other and we quickly became friends.

He had been in Auschwitz since the summer of 1944. Because of his blond hair and blue eyes, he and his brother had been able to hide in one friend's house after another in Lodz until finally they were captured just a few months ago and sent to Auschwitz. He too wanted to go to Palestine. He had trouble walking, because his wooden clogs had created huge blisters on his feet and they had become infected. He could barely hobble along. Father had managed to get us soft material to go inside our shoes so that they didn't rub. This may have saved our lives on the march.

We slept outside, when allowed to sleep, covered only by the blankets we carried. We were still in our prison uniforms, nothing more, even though it was only around thirty degrees and it often snowed or sleeted. At night it went down to five or ten degrees. After a week we finally moved into a town and were loaded onto this train. Town folks looked right through us as if we didn't exist. German civilians stood on the platforms, waiting for trains. At least half, perhaps more, of our original number had been left behind on the roads, dead. When we got onto the trains, somehow Peter was put into a different car. I hoped we would meet up again wherever we were going.

The train chugs through Germany, heading west toward the Weimar region. We travel for days, again with almost no food. Both Father and I have become very weak. Finally we are ordered off the train and are met by prisoners who assure us that we will be taken to have real showers and warmer clothes.

We are marched to the camp. We pass through a gate over which a sign proclaims TO EACH HIS DUE. We are led to a building to be disinfected. There we are forced to strip and leave all our precious possessions behind. Father and I reluctantly part with our bowls, spoons, knives, and the warm cloth in our boots. And then we are put into a room to wait. We wait forever, it seems. Some faint. Finally we are moved into another room, where we are shaved and again subjected to the torture of disinfectant thrown on our cut skin. Then a warm shower and new clothes. We are given jackets along with shirts, and I am grateful for this small mercy. Next we are lined up and registered. When it is his turn, Father makes sure he stresses all the different kinds of work he can do. I do the same. I even tell them I am a photographer.

"Where are we?" I ask the inmate who takes down the information.

"Buchenwald," he replies.

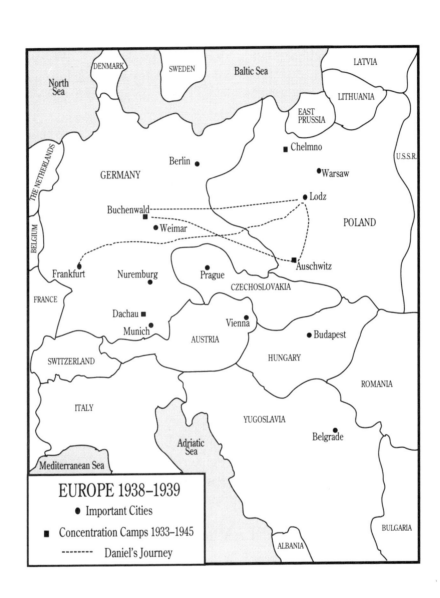

North
Sea

DENMARK

SWEDEN

Baltic Sea

LATVIA

LITHUANIA

EAST
PRUSSIA

■ Chelmno

THE NETHERLANDS

GERMANY

Berlin ●

●Warsaw

U.S.S.R.

Buchenwald ■

● Lodz

BELGIUM

● Weimar

POLAND

Frankfurt ●

Nuremburg

Prague ●

■ Auschwitz

FRANCE

Dachau ■

CZECHOSLOVAKIA

Munich ●

Vienna ●

● Budapest

SWITZERLAND

AUSTRIA

HUNGARY

ROMANIA

ITALY

YUGOSLAVIA

Belgrade ●

Adriatic
Sea

Mediterranean Sea

BULGARIA

ALBANIA

EUROPE 1938–1939

● Important Cities

■ Concentration Camps 1933–1945

-------- Daniel's Journey

PART FOUR

PICTURES OF BUCHENWALD

13

Again I am sitting on a train. It is not a freight car. It is not an open wagon. I sit on a seat. I gaze out the window at the scenery flashing by. It's spring, and I have just turned eighteen. And once more I decide to go through my pictures to organize everything so I can remember. This time some of the pictures are in my head. Some I hold in my hand. The first ones are those in my head.

The first picture I see is the large hall where we were taken after our arrival at Buchenwald. We were fed some soup and told we would stay there for three weeks of quarantine. In a way this wasn't such a terrible time. We were fed, if little, we didn't have to work, and it was not too cold in the room because of all the bodies. Peter was there and we spent much of the time talking, telling each other our stories. We gained back a little of our strength. When we were finally put into the regular camp, it was an unpleasant shock.

The inmates in our barracks were very rough, and every night there were terrible fights between the Ukrainians and the Poles. We discovered that this was the camp where most political prisoners were sent—the communists and socialists Hitler hated so much. Quickly Father tried to organize jobs for us.

One day we were both called to the main camp. I see photo after photo in my head. The Nazis had created a little paradise for themselves with grassy parks, beautiful lodges, even a zoological garden filled with pampered animals. It was quite unbelievable to see such beauty amid the squalor of the barracks. Father was put to work in a carpentry workshop, making ornate furniture for SS men. I was taken to a photography studio, where I was ordered to take photos of guards and their families on request. An older inmate ran the studio, and he needed an assistant. His name was Karl and he was a political prisoner, not a Jew. He'd been in Buchenwald since 1939. He was a communist and, I found out later, a member of the resistance in Buchenwald. Buchenwald did have a crematorium to burn the many that died of disease, torture, medical experiments, and so on, but it was not a killing center like Auschwitz/Birkenau. Nevertheless men died quickly there from the terrible conditions.

I can see the picture of the first clients who came into our studio shortly after I arrived. There was a tall fair SS man, with his tall blonde wife and their two blonde, blue-eyed children. The children, both girls, were dressed in frilly white dresses—probably stolen from some poor dead Jewish families, I thought—the mother in a stylish blue dress and high heels, the father in his SS uniform. They arranged themselves smartly for the camera and followed Karl's instructions to the

letter. They looked so content, so well fed, the model of
a perfect family. The father kissed the children
pleasantly when the pictures had been taken. The
model father.

Later that day I was running an errand for Karl, going to pick up some chemicals he needed from another
building. A young boy—he couldn't have been more
than thirteen—was sweeping the walkway. The SS officer whose picture Karl had just taken informed the
boy that he'd missed a piece of dirt. The child ran to
sweep it up. The SS man shot him in the leg. With a
cry the child fell forward.

"Get up and keep working!" the officer yelled.

The child dragged himself up and continued to
sweep. The officer shot him in the other leg.

"Get up, get working, you lazy idiot!" the officer
screamed.

The child tried, but obviously he couldn't get up.
The officer emptied his gun into the child's body.

I was frozen to the spot just behind them, my whole
body trembling with both anger and fear. I knew very
well that I could be next. And in fact, he did turn and
see me.

"Clean that up," he ordered as he walked off.

The loving father, two children of his own. And yet
he was capable of that. I felt so sick, I thought I would
vomit, but before I could do anything, two camp kapos
rushed out and took the body away, leaving me standing there in the street. I quickly came to my senses
and ran to get the chemicals for Karl. When I got
back, I told him what I'd seen. I was so distraught that
I lost all sense of caution and told him of my use of
photography at Auschwitz.

"Well, well," he said, "I'm glad to hear that, Daniel.

There is plenty of work here for those who want to be part of the resistance. You and your father could be very useful. You say you are good at taking apart machinery and the like?"

"My father and I can put together or take apart almost anything," I said.

"What is your barracks number?" he asked.

"Thirty-four."

"Be waiting outside, after everyone is asleep. Someone will come get you." He paused. "Are you willing?"

"Yes," I said. "I'll do anything."

We spent the rest of the day taking pictures of perfect German families.

14

This photo is clear in my mind. Out of the dark rises the specter of bricks, wood, shadows in the moonlight. Spirits seem to pass in and out of these shadows, the walls seem to shrink as time goes on.

Father and I waited as instructed, outside our barracks. Soon a kapo came to fetch us. We slipped in and out of the shadows. He always seemed to know where the guards would be and how to avoid them. We arrived at a building site in the main camp. The kapo whispered to us.

"That fellow over there has tools. You are to dismantle anything you can find."

We went over to the man with the tools. He gave us small flashlights as well.

"They have decided to build a gas chamber here," he whispered to us. "The Allies are very close. We can't let them do it."

Father and I each took a hammer, and we slowly and methodically began to take the nails out of the boards and lay them on the ground. We worked for around two hours before being taken back to our barracks. Twice we had to hide behind huge piles of materials as German guards checked the site. We both kept as many nails and small bits of materials as we could, to barter later. Father had already developed a busy trade with the SS. In exchange for warm clothes and food, he made them beautiful pieces of small furniture, ornate chairs and tables. They sent these back to their families for their homes. Often, though, he had somehow to find his own materials, so these nails were very valuable to him.

At work the next day Karl said, "How did it go?"

"Very well," I replied. "I would do anything," I added, "to make sure that a gas chamber is never built here."

"Fortunately most of the workers feel the same way," he replied. "They realize that they are building their own death. They work very slowly during the day, although they make it seem as if they are working furiously hard. Then we dismantle it at night. At this rate it'll never get built before the Allies get here."

"Do you have a radio?" I asked.

"Of course." He grinned. "Would you like to come and listen one night?"

I told him that I would, and so one evening after work he arranged for me to accompany him to a small hut. There a group of five men sat around a radio, and I was able to listen to the BBC for the first time in months. Was it only months ago that I had been taken to Auschwitz? It felt like I had left Lodz years ago. But now it was February 1945 and the Allies were close.

So close. Would they get to us in time to save us?

"Don't worry," one of the men said, "we have plans. We won't let them kill us all just before the Allies get here. We have some weapons. We'll fight if we have to."

That reassured me a bit. The prospect that terrified me most was being shot by the Nazis the day before our liberation.

Now I see picture after picture of the camp. If only I could have had my camera to take pictures of what I witnessed. Buchenwald was a concentration camp with factories, its purpose forced labor rather than mass extermination. Everyone worked fourteen hours a day. There was roll call every morning. Sometimes we would have to stand for hours in the early morning as they counted and recounted us. I see someone being taken away because he is missing a button on his jacket. He is shot. I see a man beaten almost to death because he did not salute an SS officer. I see seven young men, Poles, who tried to escape. They were tied to their cots and fed nothing but salt water. Their screams echoed throughout the camp for three days, until the screams became moans and they died. I see the children from the medical facilities, wandering in the grounds. Karl told me that all kinds of horrible experiments were done on them, and on adults, too. They all died eventually.

I see the luxury and opulence of the living quarters of the SS who ran Buchenwald. Often Karl and I would be ordered to take pictures in a lodge or the zoological gardens. The wealth and lavishness was astonishing.

I see the tent cities set up for prisoners outside the main camp.

I see the concert the children gave. They sang beautiful, moving songs, and the SS sat in the front row and didn't react. Perhaps they didn't understand. The children sang in Polish, German, Russian—and I saw that the human spirit was not dead. Not yet.

Somehow Father and I struggled through March. My official job at the studio came to an end because everything in the camp was becoming chaotic. The Allies were close; the Germans knew it was all over. They no longer had time to come to the studio and pose for pictures. In fact, the last thing they wanted was proof, in the form of photos of them in uniform, that they had been at Buchenwald. Many of them were taking the rank insignia off their uniforms or dumping their uniforms altogether.

Karl gave me a camera, though, and told me to take pictures of whatever I could so there would be a record. He gave me the camera on my eighteenth birthday—as a present.

I look at the picture in my hand. It was April 2. I managed to take it from the window of my studio. Rows of Jewish prisoners being marched out of Buchenwald. Perhaps to their immediate death. Perhaps to other camps.

"Why are you letting this happen?" I demanded of Karl, who was a member of the camp resistance group, one of its organizers, in fact.

"The Germans ordered we supply them with forty-five hundred Jews," he replied. "We're not strong enough to fight them yet. There are three thousand guards here."

"You didn't even try," I scoffed. "You don't care about us any more than the SS does."

"That's not true," Karl replied. "To us everyone is equal."

"Of course," I replied sarcastically, "I believe you."

April 4 was Passover, the celebration of the liberation of the Jews from Egypt, where pharaoh kept them
as slaves thousands of years ago. That night a group of
religious Hasidic Jews held a seder in our barracks
where they chanted the Haggadah by heart. Everyone
who could crowded around, and somehow the memory
of past suffering, and the fact that our ancestors had
survived it, gave us courage to try to survive our
present suffering. The service always ends with "Next
year in Jerusalem," and that line rang throughout the
barracks as we all said it as a prayer for ourselves and
for each other. Still, on April 6, another 8,000 were
marched out, non-Jews as well as Jews.

Shortly after that we could hear the fighting as it
passed very close to us. Planes buzzed overhead, can-
non shells and artillery fire exploded near the camp.

"The Americans are going after the escaping SS,"
Karl told me. "They seem to have forgotten about us
here. Come to the hut tonight. We're organizing a
rebellion. We won't just let the Nazis massacre us all."

That night we were each given a firearm to hide.
On April 10 we were all driven from our barracks and
massed in the courtyard for evacuation. I wondered
how I was to get to my gun. I had hidden it in the studio after Karl had showed me how to use it. I was sure
we would be massacred without getting a chance to
fight, when suddenly the air-raid siren wailed and the
Germans returned us to the barracks so they could
head for cover. They were scared; you could see it in
their faces.

Father and I did not return to the barracks. On in-
struction, we hid in the studio. The next morning the
Nazis again got everyone together for evacuation.
Father and I were told to hide near the gates. Our job

was to disarm or kill the guards there. Our signal was the first explosion of a grenade.

We crouched behind a building near the gate. My heart pounded. I was sweating so much, the gun felt slippery in my hands. And yet I felt happy. A feeling I hadn't had in so long—I couldn't even remember when. It would soon be over one way or another. I really didn't mind if I died like this, fighting. And if I lived, they would be *our* prisoners.

An explosion ripped through the camp. The two guards at the gate whirled around, guns pointed in our direction. Father and I shot. They fell. The guard in the tower began to fire. Father cried out and clutched his arm. I raised my gun and shot. The guard fell from the tower with a scream.

"Father, are you all right?"

"Yes, it's just my arm. Careful now, you must check the guards and get their guns."

Cautiously I moved toward them. One was dead. One was breathing heavily, blood pouring from a wound in his side. He looked up at me. "Help me," he said.

"Why?" I answered. "I'm just a filthy Jew. You wouldn't want my help."

Father had moved up behind me.

"Tie a cloth around his wound, Daniel," he said. "Every live Nazi is one more we can put on trial."

I did what he said. I'm not proud of my reaction, but the hatred and triumph I felt at that moment were stronger than any feeling of kindness.

"Daniel," my father said to me as I tied the German's wound, "we are not like them. If they've made us into them, they've succeeded."

"I know," I replied. But still I would have liked to

have shot them all. And seen them suffer first.

"Come on, Father," I said. We went into the camp. It was all over, and so quickly, it was hard to believe. The SS were surrounded and held in barracks, or had run away, too scared to fight. The prisoners had control of the camp!

A white flag made out of a tattered bed sheet was being raised on the flagpole so that the Americans wouldn't come in shooting.

"There is something I have to do," I said to Father, who was being cared for by a prisoner who was a doctor.

I left him and went looking for my model SS officer. I found him in his house, a prisoner with a gun guarding him.

"May I speak with him?" I asked his guard.

"Of course," the man replied.

Gun in hand, I rushed over to one of the little girls and picked her up.

"Don't worry," I whispered in her ear. "This is only pretend."

She nodded and seemed unafraid.

"No!" screamed her mother.

"The little boy you shot to death, he had just as much right to live as your child," I said quietly, all my rage pouring out. "A life for a life?" I waited a moment, but the officer didn't flinch. Then I put the child down and pointed the gun at the SS man's head. Fear sprang into his eyes. And his daughter began to cry.

"I'll be there to testify at your trial," I promised the officer. Then I left.

What did I think I could accomplish with that? Teach them something? It was foolish and stupid and mean. They would never learn. They would always believe that our lives had been worthless and that they were not murderers, just simple folks carrying out orders to wipe out a subhuman species. I stalked away feeling dirty and miserable.

When I got back to my father, he smiled at me and motioned me over to him. With his good arm he gave me a hug.

"It's over, Daniel," he said. "It's over."

And then I realized that he was right. We were free. And alive. I sank down beside him, unable to feel anything but an immense sense of relief. Perhaps happiness would come later.

15

I look at the next picture in my hand. It is of an American soldier, white teeth gleaming, smiling into the camera.

The night of our uprising, Father and I slept in the hospital complex. All around us were signs of Nazi brutality and viciousness. Body parts floated in bottles, needles filled and ready for use in executions lay neatly on a table. A prisoner who had worked there said the doctors prepared these needles every morning, and as the day progressed, orderlies injected the inmates. Charts showing the results of hideous experiments lay in piles. Everything was orderly and efficient, just like the Nazis themselves. And these men had called themselves doctors.

Father's wound was not serious. The bullet had not lodged in the bone, but whizzed through the fleshy part of his arm. The first thing he asked for was a shower. When he was clean, they disinfected the wound and wrapped it in clean gauze. We found SS rations—white bread and soup with meat and vegetables.

"Daniel," Father warned, "you may eat only a little. After the diet we are used to, this rich food could make us seriously ill."

It was hard to listen, but Father's advice and ingenuity had kept us alive so far, and I figured it would be senseless to get ill now.

I found a mirror and looked into it. Who was this tall, gaunt boy with large blue eyes who stared back at me? It was like looking at a stranger.

When I woke up the next morning, having slept in a cot by myself instead of with five others, I had the most amazing feeling. It was then I realized that I was truly free. I let out a whoop that scared all the others in the room half to death. I couldn't leap up; I was too weak. But I stood and screamed. "We're free! Free!" I hugged my father and everyone else in the room. And told my father I would be back to check on him later. There was something I had to do.

I ate a bit of bread and took some cheese with me and then started on my way. The camp was filled with men celebrating and with those still dying. Men and boys who were nothing but skeletons shuffled around. I had given away my food before I had gone far. Bodies lay on the ground. I headed for the camp gate. I had to walk through it, walk out of the camp, to prove to myself that this was all real. I got to the gate and moved through it. The scene before me was beautiful.

The camp was on the slope of a mountainside. All around me hills and woods stretched out in a magnificent panorama. Cherry blossoms were in bud. The grass was a deep green. The birds sang. The wind was warm on my cheeks. I couldn't help but cry. Such a beautiful world. And look what mankind had done to it.

I fetched my camera from the studio and spent the next few weeks photographing everything I could. The soldier in this picture was one of the first Americans who arrived at our camp that night. There was such cheering and yelling and celebrating—to everyone in the camp and to me, the Americans were the most beautiful sight in the entire world. Some of them cried when they saw what we had endured. All of them emptied their pockets. We were constantly showered with chocolate, gum, cigarettes. They were wonderful.

Other pictures are not so pretty. They show walking skeletons, men too weak to survive, who died in the thousands over the next few weeks. They show pits full of corpses and huts filled with dead bodies. They show camp guards on their knees begging to be set free. They whined that they had just been following orders, that they were innocent, even that they had helped Jewish friends.

Here is a picture of a farmhouse not far from Buchenwald. Karl had made me part of the militia that ran the camp. We were sent out into the countryside to round up supplies. In the meantime the Americans trucked in civilians from the area and forced them to witness the atrocities they had condoned, bury the dead, and clean up the camp. Unfortunately many in the camp continued to die—some from eating too much of the rich food, most because they were too weak to regain their health. The local people actually complained about our taking supplies from them—the local people who for eight years had pretended that Buchenwald did not exist.

I got stronger by the day. And all I wanted to do was go back to Lodz and see Rosa and to try to find

Erika and Friedrich. I found Peter and we talked about returning to Lodz together. Father, of course, wanted to find Erika. But how? He decided he would go to Lodz with me first, and then we would go to Frankfurt. Perhaps Erika would return to Frankfurt. Perhaps she was still alive.

And so here I sit on the train. It is May and we are on our way to Lodz. I am much stronger now. I am clean and dressed in clothes that are not lice infested. Peter sits beside me. Father across the way. We don't talk much. We are all thinking about those we love. Are they alive? Who has survived? How much more suffering is in store for us? I have never before now even entertained the possibility of Rosa's being dead. But of course she could be. She could have been captured and shot. Or sent to Auschwitz. Father is thinking that Erika could be dead too. And he is feeling the pain of Mother's death. He had no time to grieve before. Now it seems that as our bodies grow stronger, the pain flows through us and over us and sometimes we are nothing but pain. Tears come constantly, and when least expected.

The last few weeks in the camp, when we kept so busy helping in its running, taking part in the celebrations, the concerts, meeting with foreign delegations who suddenly wanted to know all about concentration camps, we had no time to grieve. But now we do. And it hurts.

We reach a small town in Poland and the train comes to a stop. "Half an hour before we leave," the car attendant announces.

"Come on," says Peter, "let's stretch our legs."

I grab my camera, which is always with me, and we leave the train. We take a deep breath as we stand on the platform and look around to see if there's a small market where we can buy some fresh fruit. We walk to the edge of the platform.

Suddenly coming from behind the station are four huge Polish farm boys. Of course, Peter speaks perfect Polish, and I understand a fair amount after having lived in Lodz for so long.

"What have we got here?" one of them says. "Two Jews who escaped the gas?"

I know we are in serious trouble. Even if we were both fit and healthy, these lads could make mincemeat out of us. In our present condition we don't stand a chance. I start to back away. But one of them grabs Peter, and before I can do anything, he punches him hard, in the stomach. People from the train are milling around, but no one comes to our aid.

"Stop it!" I scream, lunging at the one who threw the first punch.

One of the thugs grabs me, another punches me hard across the jaw. My whole head is ringing and I slump forward, only to be punched in the stomach. Peter is on the ground, and I can see that they are kicking his head.

"Help us!" I cry, but no one moves. I try to get loose from the grip of my captor, but I can't, so I go limp and pretend to fall unconscious. Peter is being hit mercilessly. The two who were busy with me go to beat him as he continues to struggle. He is calling them names.

"You Nazis! You pigs!"

I reach into my inner pocket and put my hand on my gun. I had resolved at the camp never to be a victim again. I roll over, take out the gun, and fire at one of the thugs. He clutches his leg and drops. I get up to my knees. Another one looks like he is going to come after me.

"Come on!" I scream. "I want to shoot you. You murderers. I want to!"

They begin to back off. Father comes pushing his way through the crowd. And finally a policeman approaches.

"Get this man to a hospital," I scream at the policeman. Peter is bleeding from the head, the mouth. He is unconscious now, barely breathing.

The policeman runs over to the Pole who is shot in the leg.

"Not him!" I scream. But they don't care. They've murdered us all and they still hate us and it still isn't enough, it is never enough.

"Get him some help," I scream, "now, or I'll shoot every single person here! And I mean it."

The policeman runs. Soon he is back with a doctor. The doctor takes in the scene and kneels by Peter. He feels his pulse, looks at his head.

"It is bad," he says. "There is probably internal bleeding. There's nothing I can do for him here. You'll have to take him to the hospital in Lodz. Maybe they can help him."

"But that's well over two hours away," Father protests.

"I can bind his head wounds, that's all," the doctor replies. "He needs an operation."

I feel like killing them all. To die now, like this, after it's all supposed to be over.

I hear a scream. It's one of pure anguish, pure anger, pure suffering. It is coming from me.

Father comes over to me. "Daniel, we'll take him on the train. That's all we can do."

I point the gun at the three remaining thugs, who now look worried. After all, crazy people shoot.

"Carry him into the train," I order, my voice shaking. "And if you drop him, I'll shoot you through the heart."

They carry him onto the train, and in time the train pulls out. Peter is stretched across two seats. I sit on the floor beside him and hold his hand and talk to him.

"Don't die now, Peter. Please. Perhaps your brother is waiting for you. Perhaps even your father and mother. You mustn't give up hope. You mustn't."

He can't die, I say to myself. He can't. Not now.

It seems to take forever to get to Lodz. Finally we arrive. The conductor has ordered ahead for an ambulance. Father and I ride with Peter to the hospital. It is crowded, but they attend to him quickly and take him into the operating theater.

We wait for hours. When the surgeon comes out, he speaks to us bluntly. "The boy suffered internal damage. We sewed him up where we could, but he'd lost a lot of blood and he's very weak. The head injury is severe. He's in a coma and we don't know if he'll come out."

"We have to find his family," I say to Father.

Father nods. "If he has any family left."

16

"Doctor," a nurse calls. "It's the young boy from surgery. I'm afraid we're losing him."

"Excuse me," says the doctor, turning to follow her.

"Please," I beg, "let me see him."

"All right," the doctor agrees. "Come with me."

Father and I follow the doctor into the intensive-care ward where Peter lies. I hurry over to Peter and hold his hand. It is cold. And then he opens his eyes and stares into mine.

"Find my family," he whispers. "Tell them."

"I will, Peter," I promise.

"You go to Palestine for me."

"I will."

"Remember . . ."

And then he sighs and closes his eyes. The nurse listens to his heart and feels his pulse. She shakes her head. I sink down to the floor and weep. I cry as if my heart will break. Not just for Peter. For all of us, left without our families, without a country to live in, left alone and broken to somehow carry on with our lives. Father comes and puts his arms around me. I cling to him like I am a baby, my head on his chest, sobbing.

Finally he pulls me up.

"I'll stay here," he says. "This boy will have a proper funeral," he vows. "He won't be thrown into a nameless grave. I'll arrange it somehow. And I'll go to the authorities to see if I can locate any of his family. In the meantime I think you have someone you want to find."

I nod.

"We'll meet back here at the front entrance at six o'clock," Father says. I nod again and make my way out toward the street.

I don't know the city of Lodz—I knew only the ghetto—so I must ask directions. At Buchenwald we were given free train passes for travel to find relatives, and they gave us some cash for our journey. I stop a young man on the street and ask him for instructions on how to find what used to be the ghetto. The streetcar takes me right up to where the old barbed-wire gates had been. I remember so well looking at these streetcars from the ghetto—especially when we used to cross the wooden bridge over the streetcar tracks. The Nazis didn't even want Jews walking on the same street Christians used, so they had built the footbridge over it. I remember a young German soldier who used to stand at the foot of the bridge and take potshots at Jews hurrying to and from work, efficiently killing all those he fired on. Where is he now, I wonder? Safely at home with his family, the murder of his innocent victims to go unpunished?

As I walk down the streets of the ghetto, I look around

and feelings wash over me. Memories. "Remember," had been Peter's last word. How will I ever forget?

Once in the ghetto, I know where to go. My heart is beating quickly. Would she have been able to leave me a note? The streets are not packed with people as they once were, but you can see that the poorer Poles have moved back into these apartment buildings. Perhaps people live in our old apartment. Perhaps . . .

And then I see her. She is sitting in front of the apartment building on a small folding chair, reading a book. Her flaming red hair gleams in the sun. She is Rosa and yet she is not. She is slim, but not the skinny waif I once knew. Her face has a healthy glow underneath her freckles. I stop and stare at her. I can't move. I am too overcome. She is alive. She is healthy. She is the most beautiful person in the entire world.

Suddenly she drops her book, turns her head, and looks directly at me as if an angel had whispered in her ear, "He's here, he's here." She stands, knocking over the chair. And then she runs; she is not smiling. She looks worried, as if she's not sure it is really me. I can't seem to move; I'm frozen to the spot. She reaches me, stops inches away, and looks up into my face. Slowly, gingerly, she raises her hand, and her slim cool fingers touch my cheek, my lips, and then I close my hands over hers and bend my head down until our lips touch and my arms are around her and I hold on to her and she to me and we are both crying, and then I pick her up and swing her in the air and we are both laughing, and then she speaks.

"These dreadful people took over your apartment, and they wouldn't even let me leave word for you with them, but I barged in and got your stuff from the cupboard and so every day for the past three weeks I've come here with my chair and a good book, and I've waited because I *knew* you'd come back, I just knew it."

And she kisses me.

"You look wonderful" is all I can think of to say.

"So do you," she replies. "You're so tall. How did you manage to grow?"

"It was all that nettle soup they fed us," I answer. "Little did they realize that it was just chock-full of vitamins and minerals and everything."

She laughs. Her laugh rings out and I feel as if it is spreading in ever-widening circles and that it will soon cover the entire continent.

"I love you," she says.

"I love you too," I answer.

And suddenly we don't know what else to say. There is so much to tell, but how much pain in the telling? We are reluctant to break this spell of pure happiness.

She runs back to fetch her book and the chair. I take the chair from her.

"My white knight," she teases.

"Always at your service, my lady."

"Come," she says, "let's get out of here."

"My pleasure."

It is a beautiful spring day, clear and mild. Rosa takes us on a streetcar to a large park. We stroll down the paths, hand in hand, until finally we sit on a bench.

The bench has a sign that reads "No Jews Allowed." We sit.

"We can't stay here," I say to her. "There is no place for us here anymore."

Rosa takes my hand.

"Palestine?" she says.

"Yes," I reply, and then hesitate before I add, "if you'll come with me."

"Is this some kind of proposal?" she says.

I sink to my knees in front of her.

"If you'll have me. If you could, if you would."

"Yes," she says.

I leap up and shout to those around, "She said yes! We're to be married!"

An old lady walking by stops and says, "God bless you. You deserve some happiness now."

"Thank you," I say.

"Sit down, Daniel," Rosa says. "I have to tell you something."

I sit. I know by the tone of her voice that this is bad news and hard to tell.

"It's about Erika."

I catch my breath.

"I saw her."

"You saw her? But where? How?"

"I started visiting the displaced persons' camps, looking for you. As you know, all the camps have compiled lists of the people in them, plus they have a master list with the names of people from other camps. At Waldenburg I saw her name. She was in the infirmary. She was very ill, Daniel."

"Go on," I urge.

"She was so happy to see me. She'd been marched to Gross-Rosen and had hidden in the infirmary the day they evacuated the camp. She simply refused to die until the Russians came and she was liberated. But then she had no more strength. I held her hand and sat with her, Daniel. I didn't leave her. I stayed with her until she died. She wanted so much to know what had happened to you and your father."

Then she pauses and looks at me, almost afraid to ask. I swipe at my tears.

"Father's alive. He's here in Lodz."

"Thank God," she says. And she adds, "I do have some good news. Friedrich made it through. He's living with us now. Part of the family, really."

"Your family?" I say. "What happened?"

"My father was killed early in the war," she says. "We found out just a few weeks ago, though. My older brother, my mother, and I. We were liberated by the Russians on January nineteenth. Three long months hiding in a cellar."

"Your little brother?"

She shakes her head. "Typhus. He caught it while we were in hiding, and we couldn't help him. By the time the Russians came, he was too weak and dehydrated to survive. But to have three members of your family alive now—why, Daniel, it's practically unheard of. We're so fortunate. So many are the only ones left. Entire families are gone." She pauses. "I don't know if it's true, but I've heard that millions of Jews were killed. Millions."

And each one a mother, or a sister like Erika, or a brother like Peter. I put my head in my hands.

"How will we have the strength to carry on?" I say.

"We will do it for all those that couldn't," she replies firmly. "We will name our children after those murdered and we will go to Palestine and help build a country. We will dedicate our lives to making sure this can never, *ever* happen again."

I look at her. I take her hand. We get up and walk together. And I know that love is a precious, precious thing, and I know that I am lucky, despite everything, to be with Rosa today.

Still, I will keep my pictures and I will tell my story. Because if we forget, we will once again be defenseless against evil. If we forget how bestial, how brutal these schoolteachers, these doctors, these professors, these clean, upstanding citizens became, if we forget, then we too could become that way. And so we shall have to learn to stop these evils before they gain power and it is too late.

I put my arm around Rosa and hold her tight as we walk. And for the moment, I am content.

Chronology

March 30, 1927—Daniel is born.

January 30, 1933—Adolf Hitler is appointed Chancellor of Germany, and the Nazi Party comes to power.

April 1–3, 1933—Germans boycott shops and businesses owned by Jews, including Daniel's father's hardware store.

September 15, 1935—The Nuremburg laws are passed to protect the "purity" of the Aryan race. Daniel's family is deprived of civil rights and the right to vote.

November 9–10, 1938—Kristallnacht, the Night of Broken Glass. Daniel's synagogue is burned, homes and business of Jews are vandalized, Jewish men and women are arrested.

September 1, 1939—World War II begins when Germany invades Poland. Curfew laws require Daniel and his family to stay in the house after nine o'clock at night.

October 18, 1941—Daniel's family is deported to the Lodz ghetto in Poland. The ghetto was first established in December 1939.

December 7, 1941—The United States enters World War II.

June 6, 1944—Allied forces land in Normandy, France, in the D-day invasion.

June 1944—Soon after D day, the Germans, afraid of defeat, order the liquidation of the Lodz ghetto. Daniel and his family are deported from Lodz to Auschwitz/Birkenau in August.

November 1944—Daniel and his father are sent from Auschwitz to Buchenwald, a concentration camp in Germany.

April 11–12, 1945—Buchenwald is liberated by American troops.

May 8, 1945—Germany surrenders to the Allies.

Glossary

Allies The countries—including the United States, Great Britain, and the Soviet Union—that opposed the Axis powers of Germany, Italy, and Japan in World War II.

Aryan The name of a prehistoric people of Europe and India. The Nazis asserted the unscientific notion that ancient Aryans had founded civilization and were racially superior and that Germans were the modern-day Aryan, or master, race. The Nazis believed that a typical Aryan was tall, blond, and blue-eyed.

Auschwitz The largest concentration camp established by the Nazis; located in Poland. See also Birkenau and Monowitz.

bar mitzvah The ceremony inducting Jewish boys into adulthood and religious responsibilities on their thirteenth birthdays.

Birkenau A segment of the Auschwitz concentration-camp complex where most of the prisoners were housed and the death camp, or killing center, was located.

Black Shirts Also known as the SS (the abbreviated form of the German for "protection squad"). Uniformed police organized in 1925 as Hitler's personal guard, and later developed into elite units of the Nazi party to operate the concentration camps.

boycott A protest in which a group of people stop buying a product or using a service, in order to express disapproval or force a change.

Brown Shirts Also known as storm troopers, or the SA (the abbreviated form of the German for "storm trooper"). Uniformed guards organized in 1920 by the Nazi Party to intimidate its opponents.

Buchenwald One of the first major concentration camps in Germany.

Chelmno The first death camp established in Poland.

communists People who believe that private property should be abolished, and that someday workers will govern themselves.

concentration camp Prison where the enemies of the German government, such as Jews, Gypsies, homosexuals, and political opponents, were gathered, or concentrated, involuntarily.

crematoria Ovens used to burn the bodies of death-camp victims.

D day June 6, 1944, the Allied invasion of Nazi-occupied Europe. This invasion marked the beginning of the Germans' eventual defeat.

Dachau The first concentration camp; established near Munich, Germany, in 1933.

death camp Camps built for the specific purpose of mass murder.

displaced persons' camp Compound administered by the Allies at the end of World War II where former concentration-camp inmates, or "displaced persons," lived, often for several years. Some displaced persons' camps were former concentration camps.

Evian conference Meeting in Evian, France, in 1938, of delegates from thirty-two nations, including the United States and Great Britain, to discuss Jewish refugees. No country offered to take in the masses of Jews wishing to escape Nazi persecution.

gas chambers Rooms, often disguised as showers, where groups of Jews and other death-camp victims were killed by poisonous gases.

Gestapo The contraction of the German words for "secret state police." Nazi political police, organized in 1933; became part of the SS (Black Shirts) in 1936.

ghetto An enclosed and restricted area of a city in which Jews were required to live.

Gypsies A nomadic people of Europe. The Gypsies, like the Jews, were persecuted by the Nazis.

Haggadah The prayer book used during the Passover Seder.

Hindenburg, Paul von 1847–1934. German general and hero of

World War I; President of Germany, 1925–34. Hindenburg was forced to appoint Hitler as Chancellor of Germany in 1933.

Hitler, Adolf 1889–1945. A founder of the Nazi Party; after 1933, Chancellor and dictator of Germany.

Hitler Youth The Nazi Party youth group for indoctrinating children and preparing them for leadership.

Kristallnacht November 9–10, 1938, the Night of Broken Glass. When synagogues across Germany were burned and Jewish-owned businesses, schools, and homes were vandalized and looted. Thousands of Jews were arrested, and some were killed.

labor camp Nazi concentration camp where inmates were used as forced laborers.

Lodz City in Poland where the first major Jewish ghetto was created by the Nazis.

Monowitz The labor-camp segment of the Auschwitz camp complex.

Nazi The abbreviated form of the German for "National Socialist German Workers' Party." Nazis preached hatred of Jews, Gypsies, homosexuals, and others, and commanded the German expansion that led to World War II.

Nuremburg laws Two German laws issued in 1935: no "impure" German could be a citizen; and no "impure" German could marry a "pure" German.

Oma German for "grandma."

Opa German for "grandpa."

Palestine A region on the east coast of the Mediterranean Sea that was the ancient homeland of the Jews. A British mandate, or territory, from 1923 to 1948, Palestine is now divided between Israel and Jordan.

Passover The Jewish holiday celebrating the Israelites' freedom from slavery in ancient Egypt.

pogrom An organized massacre of Jews.

resistance An underground organization engaged in a struggle for liberation.

SA See Brown Shirts.

Sabbath The seventh day of the week, observed by Jews from sundown Friday to sundown Saturday as a day of rest and worship. Observed by Christians usually on Sunday.

seder The ceremonial dinner held by Jews on the first evening of Passover.

socialists Followers of a theory of economics that maintains that the means of production, such as factories and mines, should be owned by the workers.

SS See Black Shirts.

Star of David A six-pointed star used as a symbol of Judaism. This symbol was the badge that the Nazis forced the Jews to wear, to distinguish them from the rest of the population.

synagogue A Jewish house of worship.

work camp See labor camp.

Yiddish A language, spoken by many European Jews, related to German and written with Hebrew characters.

Zionists Followers of the movement that arose in the late nineteenth century to restore the ancient Jewish homeland in Palestine.